In this groundbreaking work, Dave and Anna remind all educators that one must establish a first, in order to build the foundation for creating success. The other R's of Respect, Responsibility, Relevance, and Rigor will naturally flow from the connections made between teacher and student. *Caring to Teach, Teaching to Care* is an excellent resource, an inspiration, and an encouragement to anyone working with today's children and youth.
Robert Rabon, President and CEO
National Center for Youth Issues
Chattanooga, TN

The title captured my attention, but the content enlightened my heart. Every teacher should read this book to recapture the essence of education.
Kelly VanAllen, Teacher
Pine Grove ES
Orcutt, CA

Relationships matter for all those who care about children and their learning. This book reminds us that teaching is a human endeavor, and that success is achieved when the very human needs of relationship and respect are met for both students and teachers.
Shawn Lewis-Lakin, Superintendent
Manchester Community Schools
Manchester, MI

After 25 years of working in education, I appreciate the emphasis on Relationship and Relevance. While these have always been important concepts, in contemporary times they are more critical than ever. I thank the authors for putting their passions into words in ways that can inspire all of us.
Laura C. Gourlay, Counselor
Oasis High School,
Mt. Pleasant, MI

Caring to Teach, Teaching to Care provides straightforward information for novices and veteran educators. Short, concise and user-friendly, it would be a great way to begin the "conversation" during professional

development. The Classroom Exercises at the conclusion of the book offer many practical ideas of *how* to engage students in the five R's.
Christine N. Heerlein, MA, Reading Specialist
Uthoff Valley Elementary/Rockwood School District
Fenton, MO

Often educators are looking for new ways to instill good behavioral practices in children. *Caring to Teach, Teaching to Care* provides questions and activities that educators and future educators will find useful and stimulating in creating a caring community of learners—the way schools *should* be functioning.
Krystyna Nowak-Fabrykowski, Professor
Department of Teacher Education and Professional Development
Central Michigan University

As an educator and counselor of more than 30 years, I find it refreshing that *Caring to Teach, Teaching to Care* brings us back to the importance of teaching the <u>whole child</u>. This book provides educators with tools and understanding to help students develop the "five R's" as a means to create a passion for success and learning. *Caring to Teach, Teaching to Care* is an excellent resource for all who truly desire to teach.
Anne Teague, MA, LPC, NCC
Field Representative
National Center for Youth Issues

I am thrilled to see that a book has been written about the importance of refocusing on *relationship* in our educational efforts. Similar to Dave, I ended every day by giving each kindergartner a handshake or a hug. Today I am an assistant principal at a high school in that district, and former students will often approach me to ask for a handshake or a hug. This connection that was made 10-12 years ago clearly did make a difference.
Kandis Pritchett, Assistant Principal
Midland High School
Midland, Michigan

Caring to Teach, Teaching to Care

Other books by Dave Opalewski

Confronting Death in the School Family
Answering the Cry for Help: Suicide Prevention/Education for Schools and
   Communities
Understanding and Addressing Adolescent Grief Issues
Understanding and Addressing Children Grief Issues

Other books by Anna Unkovich

Chicken Soup for the Soul in the Classroom/Elementary Edition
Chicken Soup for the Soul in the Classroom/Middle School Edition
Chicken Soup for the Soul in the Classroom/High School Edition
Magic Moments: This Worked for Me

Caring to Teach, Teaching to Care

The Importance of
*R*elationship,
*R*espect,
*R*esponsibility,
*R*elevance,
and
*R*igor
in the Classroom

Dave Opalewski & Anna Unkovich

iUniverse, Inc.
Bloomington

Caring to Teach, Teaching to Care
The Importance of Relationship, Respect, Responsibility, Relevance, and
Rigor in the Classroom

Copyright © 2011 by Dave Opalewski & Anna Unkovich.

All rights reserved. No part of this book may be used or reproduced by any means, graphic, electronic, or mechanical, including photocopying, recording, taping or by any information storage retrieval system without the written permission of the publisher except in the case of brief quotations embodied in critical articles and reviews.

The names of all students and negative-impact teachers have been changed to protect their identities. In each case, we have noted the false name with an asterisk (*).

The actual names of teachers who have had a profoundly positive effect on our own lives and teaching are included. It is our intent to show our appreciation and respect, and to honor them by naming them in this book.

iUniverse books may be ordered through booksellers or by contacting:

iUniverse
1663 Liberty Drive
Bloomington, IN 47403
www.iuniverse.com
1-800-Authors (1-800-288-4677)

Because of the dynamic nature of the Internet, any web addresses or links contained in this book may have changed since publication and may no longer be valid. The views expressed in this work are solely those of the author and do not necessarily reflect the views of the publisher, and the publisher hereby disclaims any responsibility for them.

Any people depicted in stock imagery provided by Thinkstock are models, and such images are being used for illustrative purposes only.
Certain stock imagery © Thinkstock.

ISBN: 978-1-4620-2141-3 (sc)
ISBN: 978-1-4620-2142-0 (ebk)

Printed in the United States of America

iUniverse rev. date: 06/02/2011

Contents

Dedication

To the many wonderful teachers who are changing the world,
one student at a time.

You are a marvel. Each second we live is a new and unique moment of the universe, a moment that will never be again . . . And what do we teach our children? We teach them that two and two make four, and Paris is the capitol of France. When will we also teach them what they are? We should say to each of them: Do you know what you are? You are a marvel. You are unique. In all the years that have passed, there has never been another child like you. Your legs, your arms, your clever fingers, the way you move. You may become a Shakespeare, a Michelangelo, a Beethoven. You have the capacity for anything. Yes, you are a marvel. And when you grow up, can you then harm another who is, like you, a marvel? You must work—we must all work—to make the world worthy of its children.

—Pablo Casals

PREFACE

It is not our intention with this book to re-invent the wheel. Rather, it is offered as a reminder of what is important in education—our students. And, it is offered as an encouragement to refocus our efforts to make *relationship* the primary *R*, so that we are truly connecting with today's students, many of whom feel isolated and alone.

Most of our thoughts and writing come from our personal experiences in the classroom—a combined 71 years of wisdom gleaned from our own successes and failures. Occasionally, we refer to other experts we encountered who support our thoughts and mission, and have referenced them for your further consideration.

Next, we wanted to address those 3:00 a.m. "a-ha moments," where a genius thought popped into one of our minds and made it to a post-it note in the dark. Was it something read months or years ago that has now surfaced in our dreams, or a divine seed of wisdom from above? The answer to that, we do not know and cannot accurately document, but we are grateful for its place in our message to you.

Please know that we are passionate about being educators and wish for you to find as much joy in your career as we have found in ours. We hope that this book will guide you and inspire you when setting priorities in your own classrooms as well as to help you make life-long relationships with your students.

An Attitude Adjustment Courtesy of Carl Reiner

Having a friend who works in the movie industry added excitement to Anna's yearly spring break visits to California, especially when being granted access to some of the friend's bosses' unused perks.

One year, they had tickets to "An Intimate Gathering with Carl Reiner," an affair of about seventy-five writers and directors of Hollywood's inner circle. They were ecstatic! Carl Reiner, an award-winning actor, writer, director, producer, and comedian, had been a particular favorite of Anna's since she was a young girl. At the gathering, she was captivated by his inspirational and humorous message, although today, she remembers none of it.

During the reception that followed, she stood at the back of the room watching as a line of people approached Mr. Reiner to have a private word with him. Eventually, most of the crowd dispersed and she realized that this would be her only opportunity to tell this amazing man how she felt about him and his work. But, she was not "one of them." How could she even *consider* approaching this famous man?

Anna took a deep breath and moved quietly behind him before she lost her nerve. A few moments later, he turned to acknowledge her presence. She knew she had to speak—it was now or never.

"Mr. Reiner," she began. "I'm not a member of the Screen Writers Guild, and I'm not in the 'business,' and I really don't belong here. I'm **just** a teacher. But, I had to tell you how much I enjoyed your talk tonight and have loved watching you over the years."

While Anna may have forgotten the essence of his speech, she will **never** forget what happened next. Mr. Reiner pulled her to his side in a warm hug, thanking her for her kind words. Then, he turned, faced her with his hands on her shoulders, and looked her sternly in the eyes as he said, "Don't **ever** say 'just a teacher.' You have the most important job on the planet. You teach our children and influence the entire world. Don't **ever** say, 'just a teacher!'"

Since that moment, she never has!

Happiness comes from following your passion.
Excellence comes from work that you are passionate about.
Knowing what to do is certainly important, but knowing why you do it
fuels your motivation . . . your passion.
A strong passion enables you to find a way to achieve your goals . . .
any goal.
Passion turns your stumbling blocks into stepping stones.
Not only does passion ignite your pursuit of excellence,
passion also makes the journey more fun!

—David Cottrell

ACKNOWLEDGEMENTS

First, we would like to thank our editor, Jeanette Morris, for her attention to detail and her tireless handholding in this process called book publishing.

Second, our appreciation goes to Lori Block, our graphic artist, who designed this *"wow-pick-me-up"* cover.

Third, to the folks at iUniverse, we are grateful for your staff, organization, guidelines, and tutorials, which helped convert an idea into a reality.

Last, and most important, our love and gratitude go to our families and friends for their unfailing belief in us and in the importance of our work with educators; specifically, to Dave's wife, Deb Opalewski, and to Anna's husband, Don Dirkse. We could not have accomplished this dream without your support.

INTRODUCTION

A Few Words from Dave

I want to start out by stressing that Anna and I both believe in the value and importance of solid academia in our schools. These skills and this knowledge are significant to the future of our youth and of our country. However, in our efforts to put a greater influence on academic achievement, we recognize the need to ask ourselves the following questions:

- Is it possible that political pressure forces educators to achieve "average yearly progress" in a manner that loses a clear picture of our youth's lives and needs?
- Have students changed, or have there been major familial, community, and institutional changes that currently impact our youth?
- Do young people have a desire and a need to be connected with others, young and old?
- As educators, have we focused mainly on academic skills while overlooking other constructive and healthy school events, which are crucial to the social and emotional development of our young people?
- Are we viewing our students as "products," trained in labor and skills to maintain a society, rather than as the children that they are?
- Are today's student problems and needs substantially different from those faced by our schools in the recent past?
- Is it possible that in an attempt to achieve better test score results, we have lost touch with our students as people?

I strongly believe the answer to all of these questions is a resounding yes. As educators, we must increase our efforts to understand youth and their driving forces. We must truly engage with youth, connect with them, and allow them to connect with us. Education in the twenty-first century demands that we deal with the whole child, not just the mind. This requires a new focus in our schools. A wise individual once said, "Students do not care how much you know until they know how much you care." We must let our youth know that they matter to us.

Schools also need to address societal issues in a way that does not suggest that our young people are the problem. Social contexts such as familial changes, demographic differences, the rapid change of pace of daily living, and media and technology influences all have affected our youth, influencing their basic motivations, and what they really want and need. Course materials addressing such issues have been cast from our school curriculum since they cannot be measured on a test.

Sadly, the state achievement test seems to be the driving factor in establishing priorities in our schools. A test-driven classroom de-personalizes the student-teacher relationship and destroys the passion for learning. Therefore, it is imperative that we not allow these mandated, standardized tests to wholly determine what is taught, nor should educators constantly face the threat of "produce or punish."

My Classroom Wake-Up Call—Dave's Story

At one point in my career, I was transferred mid-year to teach pre-algebra to eighth graders, and immediately realized I had huge hurdles to climb. How does one make algebra *relevant* to students? Negative attitudes and perception about algebra were common:
"Algebra stinks"
"I can't do it."
"I hate this stuff!"
"I'm frustrated!"
"I get poor grades in math."
"Why do I need to learn this stuff, anyway? I'm never going to use it."

The remedy to helping students "fell into my lap" as I was demonstrating how to solve a particular equation. I had covered the process thoroughly, step-by-step. When finished, I asked for questions and one student raised his hand. Rather than asking a question, the student said, "I know another way you can solve the equation. Can I show you?"

I gladly handed the chalk to the student to proceed, delighted by the unexpected enthusiasm.

The student then solved the equation using a *different process* from the one that the text and the math department required students to use. Although different, the process used by the student made perfect sense to him and was logical. Once this boy finished at the board, three more students raised their hands. All were excited to demonstrate their methods of solving the equation.

At that point, I had a big decision to make. Should I tell the students that they had to go by the process demanded by the math department? Or, could they use their own process as long as it was logical and made sense?

I chose to allow the students to determine the process that made the most sense to them. Following that decision, the class became more enthusiastic about algebra, and their classroom behavior and effort dramatically improved. The students were clearly more able to make connections between what they were learning and their world. They were *implying* meanings and *applying* applications—the true essence of education.

This work attempts to address issues that will help our schools to develop students' minds, and will develop their *hearts* as well.

A Few Words from Anna

As Dave and I discussed the writing of this book, I wondered about the classrooms of today. What are we doing wrong that allows for:

- a 50% dropout rate in some communities? 25% nationally?
- teen suicide to be the third leading cause of death among young adults?
- "teaching to the test," or "scripted classrooms" to exist?
- students to feel isolated?
- students to consider violence, even murder, as an option in problem-solving?
- students to treat classmates and teachers disrespectfully?
- classrooms, hallways, and school buildings to be trashed and vandalized?

Without dismissing the importance of the original **3 R's**—reading, writing, and 'rithmetic—what needs to be *added* to our classroom environment to make it successful on a world level? Our belief in "education for all" does not have students clamoring to get into our classrooms, as is true in countries where only the privileged few children are educated. Our low teacher salaries and lack of respect for the profession cannot compare with our societal value for sports, and the accompanying salaries paid to athletes.

What is missing from our classrooms that can be readily found on our playing fields?

I dream of American classrooms where students can hardly wait to learn *every* lesson, or where they spend hours studying a subject on their own volition, not under threat of a test, or where teaching is a highly paid, highly valued, and respected profession that matches its importance to the coming world.

But, what can we do right now that would make a difference? The answer is summed up by emphasizing five other R's that must reside in our education system: ***Relationship, Respect, Responsibility, Relevance, and Rigor.***

From Teacher to Coach, From Coach to Teacher— Anna's story

Somewhere in the middle of my teaching career, I was *coerced* into taking a coaching position, even though I knew absolutely **nothing** about coaching, and had never been an athlete.

Since competitive sports were not an option for young women growing up in northern Michigan in the early 1960s, I grew up resenting this discrimination. And ultimately, I resented the sports, the athletes, the coaches, and the system that pampered the talented athletes and even changed the rules for them. Because God had blessed these good athletes with certain skills, they were given privileges and popularity beyond anything they had rightfully earned.

Twenty years later, with my resentments firmly entrenched, I was taken aback when I was begged to take a coaching position without qualification. "You understand kids" was the administration's response. Most surprising to me was that I accepted the challenge. I studied hard, volunteered at track and field or cross-country camps and competitions at every opportunity. I became a good coach.

What does this have to do with five other Rs in education? Everything.

1. I was asked to take the position because I already had a good **Relationship** with my students. It was a heart-to-heart connection. I cared about them, so they cared about what I was teaching them.
2. Every athlete was treated with **Respect**—from the first place winner to the last place finisher. Every athlete was expected to cheer for teammates in *every* event. They didn't have to love each other on or off the field, but they were expected to look out for each other, and to work together at all times, as a team, as a family kind of unit.
3. I considered every athlete who put on a uniform to be a potential *hero* to a teammate, or a younger child. These athletes were expected to act like heroes at all times, and to take full **Responsibility** for their grades, their classroom

behavior, their behavior in any school areas and activities, as well as their conduct in the community and on the track.

4. Everything we did to prepare for competition was **Relevant** to these young men. They could see the connection between their efforts and their successes.

5. I challenged them, teased them, taunted them, and taught them the importance of **Rigor**. "If this old lady can do this, so can you!" (I was age 38 when I started coaching). We trained hard! We did pool workouts and mind training; we studied nutrition and did endless warm-ups and cool-downs. I monitored their grades all year long, not just during our season. They knew that school came first, and sports followed, no matter how great their skill. Essentially, we did the things that Olympians were doing, only we did them as seventh, eighth, and ninth graders.

The results came quickly. We became city champs, and had undefeated seasons year after year. The most powerful thing is that those five **R's** allowed me to do more **teaching** on and off the playing field than I ever could have accomplished in my classroom alone.

Our goal with this book is to show the importance of moving those *five R's* into every classroom in America. Until we realize our dream of America viewing teaching as a highly respected and well-paid profession, this is something we can do right now.

Please enjoy the journey as we explore the other *five R's*.

Part One

Defining the Problem

Chapter 1

A Sense of Urgency

Social-Emotional Illiteracy

Someone once stated, "As educators, teaching children isn't as much what we do as who we are."

From this statement, two important beliefs can be inferred:

- Children are our country's most precious resources.
- Educators can and do touch the future by making positive differences in the lives of children.

A major question then follows: "Does the present state of education in our country reflect these two important beliefs?"

It is easy to point the finger at parents for not having their children "learning ready" as they enter preschool or kindergarten. It is similarly easy to place blame on parents for a void in children's emotional development, lack of values, and social skills.

Although many parents do a stellar job in raising their children, educational institutions are not excused from their responsibility to help develop every child's heart as well as his or her mind. In fact, The Search Institute, an independent, nonprofit, nonsectarian organization whose mission is to advance the well-being of adolescents and children, lists developmental assets that children need to become emotionally healthy. Three of these assets should be of particular interest to all educators:

Asset #3—"Children need support from three or more non-parent adults."

Most of these adults tend to be teachers.

Asset # 5—"A caring school climate."

The school environment needs to be caring and encouraging for all students.

Asset # 24—"Bonding to school."

The young person feels a connection with and cares about his/her school.[1]

From these three assets, it can be concluded that children coming either from sound homes or from troubled homes need the emotional and social developmental skills provided by schools. One can further deduce the role that schools must play in developing the whole child, in every child.

There is no value in assigning blame, yet the following questions need to be asked:

- Is our present educational system guilty of not meeting children's needs by focusing on demands forced on it by the "No Child Left Behind" legislation?
- With so much emphasis and concentration on getting students to pass a state assessment test, are educators failing to present students with opportunities to develop healthy emotional and social skills?
- Are schools failing to develop a sense of community in the classroom and school environments?

Although academic knowledge and skills are very important, the focus seems to be on only developing children's minds, with little, if any, time left for developing their *hearts*. As a result, opportunities have become rare for children to learn about and discuss social and emotional issues facing them in the classroom and in the world. This lessens the chance for children to become emotionally healthy, well rounded, and productive citizens.

Statistics Point to Problems

The following list of recent statistics can be strong evidence for this point:

- Research has found that 80% of students entering school felt good about themselves.[2]
- Only 20% continue to do so after the fifth grade.[3]
- 62% of U.S. adolescents claim that suicide is a common thought to them.[4]
- Suicide has increased 124% in the 10-14 age group in the last ten years.[5]
- The high school dropout rate was approximately 20% at the ending of the 2007-2008 school year. In 2010, it was at 25%.[6]
- High school dropouts are more likely to be involved in crime.[7]
- It is estimated that 10 million females in the U.S. have eating disorders.[8]

The point must be made that this is a short list of issues facing our children. Problems such as bullying, divorce, parental unemployment, abuse, poverty, as well as the more global topics such as: war, the economy, discrimination, and climate change are just some of the things that affect our youth and create the need for providing healthy emotional development opportunities for them.

In 1983, Rudolph Flesch authored *Why Johnny Can't Read*.[9] This book was a shocking wake-up call for educators and parents. It brought to light that our society was quickly becoming illiterate, and there would be a devastating price to pay if things didn't change. The concept of "five additional R's" presented in this book is a wake-up call of equal or even greater proportions. One must ask: of what value will knowledge be if, as a society, we are emotionally unstable and socially uncooperative? We cannot and should not try to separate the mind from the heart.

The Urgency

The urgency of this issue comes from far more than the statistics presented here. The prevailing attitude that education is not important, that it is not worthy of time or money spent, that *anyone can teach*, that inherently it has no real value—this attitude of worthlessness has been with us for centuries. It is like a virus permeating all of society and now reaching epidemic proportions. And, like any virus, although unseen by the naked eye, it is slowly and equally destructive.

The societal and political microscope that is finally examining this virus seems to turn to old ways of solving the problem: more testing and higher graduation requirements, particularly in math and science. What good is there in demanding these requirements if students refuse to stay in school in the first place? What about the *value* of literature, art, music, physical education, or the social sciences? How often is the worth of these fields of endeavor diminished by the emphasis placed on math and science alone? *If we always do what we've always done, we'll always get what we always got.*

Education must change its focus from the head to the heart. Teachers must first connect with students, heart to heart, before true learning can take place. Good education begins on a two-way street of caring, then of learning.

Finding Solutions

Again, this is not an issue of blame. It is an opportunity for solution. Educators must believe that they can be a positive factor in helping children deal with their issues and develop resiliency skills. Just as quality environments lead to healthy lives, quality educational environments lead to lifelong educational opportunities for children.

The good news is that teachers already have the tools they need to create quality classroom environments, which will develop children's hearts as well as their minds. No requisitions have to be filled out; no money needs to be spent. New curriculum or elective classes need not be designed and forced into the existing school week.

The tools to effect quality classroom environments are inherent in the character of educators. As a profession, they are people who love children and adolescents and who are dedicated to their happiness and success in the classroom and in life. What might be lacking, but can be reignited, is a strong sense of urgency in getting the focus back on developing the whole child, emotionally and socially, as well as academically.

The answer to our failing education system lies in *how* students are taught more than *what* they are taught.

Chapter 2

Three R's to Eight R's:
What's Needed, Why Now?

School Sets the Tone for a Lifetime of Learning

The three R's that began with our country's educational system over 200 years ago, or that is exemplified in the following story of 50 years ago, seemed to be adequate for the times. While each set a tone for a lifetime of learning, one must ask if Reading, Writing, and Arithmetic are enough to meet the needs of students today.

Real Stories: A Chapter a Day . . . A Lifetime of Learning

Mrs. Ferguson taught grades three through six in a rural school in the fifties and sixties. She started each day with a chapter from the *Little House on the Prairie* book series. Many of her students could hardly wait to get to school to see what was happening with Laura and the other children, and were most fascinated by the school experiences of students in the nineteenth century. In addition to making American history come alive, those stories created a lifetime love of reading and learning for many of her students.

Three R's in the History of Education

The main subjects in school during Laura Ingalls' day in the 1800s were the **three R's**—reading, writing, and 'rithmetic, with some history and geography added for the older students. School was a place of memorization and recitation, with the teacher as the only real resource in the room. Most likely, she was a single woman who had been a good student herself. She moved from student role into that of teacher with little or no formal training.

Reading was synonymous with *McGuffey's Fifth Eclectic Reader,* which was most likely the only textbook in the classroom. All students were expected to read aloud from this text and to memorize grammar rules, spelling words, and verses of poetry or adages such as "a stitch in time saves nine."

Writing lessons consisted of practice at cursive penmanship, perhaps rewriting a poem, or a chapter from the Bible. **'Rithmetic** consisted of memorization of tables and "doing sums" or other simple math calculations.

One room, one teacher, all subjects, all grades. The teacher was in full control of the content and pace of each of her students' learning. Often, older students would help tutor younger students. The teacher's only break in the day was when students went outside for unsupervised recess where hide-and-seek, tag, or Simon Says might have been played. Character development, morals and ethics, prayer, and Bible readings were a normal part of the classroom day in the nineteenth century.

Societal Impact on Learning—Then . . .

In the 1800s, the family unit was strong, divorce was unheard of, and the family was the key socializing agent. Children were valued for their labor, their ability to help farm the land, or their contribution to the family welfare. Household tasks were dictated by gender and age. Roles were clearly defined within the family: men went to work and did the outdoor chores; women stayed home, did the indoor tasks, and raised the children.

The elements were harsh and resources were minimal, so survival was always at the forefront. This forced even the most reserved or reticent to rely on neighbors and others in the community for support. One's very survival depended on the human-to-human connections that were maintained.

Women as teachers seemed to be the exception to the roles stated above, but only for single women. Often, by written contract, these women were forbidden to date or to marry. If they did, they would be fired from their teaching positions.

Little changed in the twentieth century classroom until the late 1960s, although the restriction for female teachers to remain single was lifted as women became more vocal and insistent upon equal rights.

And Now . . .

Fast-forward to education today in the twenty-first century. Teachers are not automatically respected or revered. Quite the contrary. At the very least, teachers must earn the respect of their students. And, in many cases and communities, teachers are often disrespected simply because of their authoritative position. Parents no longer automatically back the teacher in disciplinary action, but often challenge teachers' decisions in a misguided attempt to protect their children. They may succeed in glossing over their child's record, but in the end, the lesson of entitlement taught to the student is powerful and damaging to the child and to society at large.

Most American classrooms today are student-centered. Even the placement of classroom desks and chairs indicates more of a community of learning, rather than a focus on the teacher.

Students are now taught more about *how* to think and *how* to learn. Even more important is knowing how to *find* information in a world where new discoveries are made every day. Memorization is minimal, recitation is unheard of, and public humiliation of students for incomplete or poorly done homework is considered abusive.

Resources abound, and teachers are not expected to know everything. Subject matter is departmentalized with each teacher specializing in specific content areas and being the "expert" on that particular subject. Some could even be "ignorant" of most of the other subjects being taught in his or her school.

With many families no longer taking the time or the responsibility to teach their children social skills, that task has fallen on the schools. Basic manners, and the words "please" and "thank you" are rarely heard. Without the efforts of the teacher to model and instruct these things, these courtesy behaviors would be lost.

In many schools, and before big budget cuts, a wide variety of extra-curricular activities have been made available in an attempt to foster the social-emotional growth of our youngsters. From sports such as swimming, football, or gymnastics, to student interest clubs such as drama, chess, or jazz ensemble, efforts have been made to reach students at every interest level.

Societal Impacts Affecting Education Today

The following is a list of some key societal impacts on education that will be addressed in the chapters that follow:

- media and technology
    computers, television, cell phones and hand-held devices
    the information highway
    high volume of violence witnessed
    problems "solved/resolved" in 30-minute segments
    "attached" to technology—less "human" connection
- family structure
    high rate of divorce
    physical, emotional, and financial challenges of divorce
    life in blended families, single-parent, or non-parent homes
    geographic distance from extended family support
    over-scheduling of activities for parents and children
- societal changes
    physical survival no longer primary
    emotional survival to the forefront
    recreation/free time expectations
    lack of respect or tolerance for human differences
    lack of "an entire village to raise a child"
    living in a high-stress, fast-paced society

- classroom changes
    - teachers' platters are over-filled
    - over-emphasis on testing, not learning
    - political stifling of the creative, joyful learning process
    - student attitude of "entitlement"
    - high action, high energy, high entertainment expectations
    - teacher-student time ratio vs. parent-student time spent together
    - teacher as the stable, adult role-model for many students
    - expectation for educators to meet *all* needs of *every* child
    - education as a *business*, building and marketing students as *products*

In looking at this list and these issues in upcoming chapters, it will be evident that these changes in society demand more from teachers than ever before—**five more R's.** While the length of the day remains at twenty-four hours, and many political leaders attempt to pile more onto teachers' platters, additional expectations for teachers is far from being the solution. Rather, it is a matter of shifting priorities in the school day.

It is becoming more evident that **relationship, respect, responsibility, relevance, and rigor** are critical to the survival and success of our contemporary students. However, that requires removal of some of the "litter" from the teacher's load in order to focus on what is important now. It is time to get politics out of the classroom and once again allow teachers to teach. It is time to increase teacher salaries in order to attract the brightest and best. It is time to encourage teacher creativity that ignites the spark of learning for our children. It is time to educate the community, the nation, even the entire world, about the importance of our teachers in changing the world, one student at a time. It is time . . .

What better "tool" to accomplish this than oneself and one's ability to make a difference with affirming words, with genuine interest, availability, and example. None of this costs a dime nor needs a requisition.

All five of these R's are important. But first, there *must* be a **relationship** with students—*a connection with them.*

Chapter 2 Thought Starters

1. Is the 3-R focus that founded our country over 200 years ago adequate for your students? Why or why not?

2. Is your classroom media dependent? Has technology made your job as a teacher easier or more complicated? Explain your current situation.

Part Two

Relationships

Chapter 3

Building Quality Relationships with Students

Classroom Relationships—Then . . .

In the nineteenth century, the relationship between teacher and student was rigidly defined. Discipline was strict. Students spoke only when called upon or after requesting permission to speak. Often, a new teacher was only a year older than some of her students, so having strict boundaries was essential.

Enforcement of rules was firm, with the slightest infraction being dealt with immediately. Students were *expected* to behave and parents fully supported that concept. Corporal punishment was a normal part of the school day—the use of a switch, a paddle, or a ruler to remind students of the rules was common. Humiliation and verbal chastisement were typical punishment for lessons not learned. Picture the "dunce" standing in the corner, facing the wall, for perhaps hours at a time.

And Now . . .

In studying schools across our county that at one time were considered to be failing, those that made 180° turns had two things in common: Improved school climate and enhanced reading skills. The original *R—Reading—*has been addressed in many other books. The focus here is to introduce you to the biggest *R* that affects school climate—*Relationship.*

Education is a people business. The sooner that teachers of every level learn this extremely important principle, the better the educational experience will be for both the child and the educator. One major component of a quality life is developing quality relationships. As quality relationships are developed with students, attitudes improve. When attitudes improve, behavior improves. When behavior improves, the classroom atmosphere for learning improves. When the classroom atmosphere for learning improves, attendance for both students and teachers improves. When attendance improves, the chance for academic success greatly improves.

The greatest needs of young people are affection, acceptance, feeling valuable, and knowing that they have a positive purpose in life. Although knowledge is of unquestionable importance, unless the educational system focuses on developing the whole child, the development of the mind will be limited. This means that schools must put energy into the social and emotional welfare of their students, as well as their physical and mental development.

If you were to walk into a typical elementary school building in America, you would almost immediately witness young children who are willing and needing to give hugs to their teachers, or any other caring adult. These children want to please because they need acceptance and assurance from the adults in their world. Children need to be valued, and they also need to *feel* valuable. The school "family" cannot totally take the place of the student's family of origin in these matters. However, educators must believe that they can, and do, make a positive difference in young people's lives when they provide a caring environment at school.

So, what has changed, necessitating a focus on **relationship** in education today? While there are many influences, this chapter will address three that are critical:

- the family structure has changed
- the world of communication has changed
- the top priorities of schools have changed

Indeed, if educators do not acknowledge these changes, and adapt to them, children today may not learn at all.

The Family Structure has Changed

According to the U.S. Census Bureau, in 1970, 2.2 million (3.2%) of American children lived in a household maintained by a grandparent. By 1997, that number rose to 3.9 million (5.5%), representing a 76% increase. More recent data on the growing number of children being raised by their grandparents show these numbers continuing to rise.[1]

Even though most of these grandparents are loving and caring, in most cases their advancing age presents challenges in communication and understanding. The wide generation gap and different "world" in which these children and adolescents are growing up poses certain problems not typically experienced by children raised by parents. Adolescence can be particularly challenging for any caregiver, but the difficulties tend to be magnified for non-parental custodians.

Another issue to consider is that the typical 62-year-old doesn't have the energy he/she had in earlier years when raising his/her own children. Additionally, grandparents may not have the patience needed to raise and be wholly responsible for these youngsters. Few grandparents want the pressure of coping with teenagers during their "golden years." It is admirable when grandparents step in to help, but one must also recognize the fact that this is a challenging situation for both the children and the grandparents.

It is now estimated that 4.5 million young people in the United States under the age of 18 are living with grandparents who are the head of the household. Several reasons are given for this shift in "parenting" onto grandparents: teen pregnancy, divorce, mental and physical illness, crime, child abuse, neglect, drug abuse of the parents, and incarceration.[2]

Here is a closer look at some of these issues:

- 44% of children who are living with grandparents are there because their parents abused alcohol or other drugs.[3] Because children don't understand the power of addiction, many believe that their parents love the drugs more than they are loved. This deep sense of rejection leads to deep hurt and this deep hurt

19

tends to manifest into anger. Over time, this anger becomes internalized. Experts claim that when this happens, there is a large chance that depression will follow. All of this can and usually does result in the child feeling unlovable and not valued.

- 28% of these children are living with grandparents because their biological parents abused or neglected them.[4] The manifestations tend to be the same as the children dealing with parental alcohol and other drug problems.
- 11% of these children are living with grandparents because of the death of one or both parents.[5] This, in itself, presents many difficult challenges for these children as they try to cope with their loss and keep up with their lessons in the classroom.

In addition to students living with grandparents, there also has been an increase in students living with other family members such as aunts and uncles, older siblings, and family friends for the same reasons.

Some Effects of Divorce on Students in the Classroom

Recent statistics cite that the parents of 41% of students will divorce.[6] Children love their parents no matter what the situation or relationship may be between them. Experiencing the divorce of parents is a time of grief and mourning for the child, even if the day-to-day living situation may improve. While the anger, and perhaps violence, may leave the household, children still experience the loss of the family as a unit and the *dream* of the "perfect family."

Most studies indicate that children of divorce can be impacted in the following ways:

- altered day-to-day living situations (changes in residence/schools)
- increased economic restrictions
- increase in daily stress
- feelings of confusion and guilt when parents lean on them for emotional support or manipulate them into "taking sides"
- lowered self-esteem
- being bribed for affection

- loss of non-custodial parent (or less availability)
- step-parent or blended family issues/conflicts

Children of divorce tend to be at **greater risk** for exhibiting:

- academic problems
- aggression or anger
- depression
- early sexual activity as adolescents
- apathy
- regression to more immature behaviors
- feelings of powerlessness
- rebellion, alcohol or other drug use

Evidence shows that not all children of divorce will experience these behaviors. Gender, age, psychological health, and maturity will affect the impact of divorce on children. In fact, only about 25% will have a noticeable reaction to the divorce of their parents. Impact is most detrimental when one or both parents abandon responsibility for their child's emotional and social welfare. According to Brian Pruit, author of *The Power of Dad,* "51% of children involved from divorced homes whose mother receives custody will only see their father once a year, or rarely ever again, one year after the divorce."[7]

The two factors having the most *positive* impact on children of divorce are:

1. parents who have a non-adversarial divorce
2. children of all ages who have a strong connection with at least one other caring adult—**usually a teacher!**

Other Issues Facing Students

A growing number of children are awakened for school by an older sibling or someone else other than their parents, even though they are living with both parents. In most of these cases, the parents are already off to work. These children seldom get a proper breakfast before they leave for school, and more importantly, they don't get that needed hug from Mom or Dad on their way out the door. The smile they get from their teacher may be the first, and perhaps only smile they get that day.

Looking at some of the statistics and stories presented here, it is evident that many children in our schools are "emotionally wounded." If educators fail to give them hope and purpose in life, who will? These felt needs can only be offered by caring adults who take the time and effort to build positive relationships. Good educators believe that the way to a child's mind is through his/her heart. To effectively educate children, teachers must develop a positive *relationship* with them. The chances for a quality education are greatly enhanced when children like coming to school, when they feel safe, and when they enjoy being in the classroom.

The World of Communication has Changed

It is impossible to address everything that mandates a need for a strong teacher-student connection. However, one additional and important concern must be addressed—technology. In spite of its advantages, technology serves to distance young people from *human* interactions.

Real Stories: Two Parents, Two Phones, One Child

A young couple was having breakfast with their 18-month-old son in a lovely bed and breakfast on the outskirts of Los Angeles.

"I don't think it's illegal, but I certainly question if it's ethical," the mother spoke into her cell phone while breaking off a piece of toast and handing it to her son.

"Well, have you gotten a second opinion?" she queried the person on the other end.

"I think that's crucial." She continued handing her son bits of toast.

On the other side of the table, the father was on *his* cell phone. "I told him to get me the info for the contract, and I would get back to him by Friday." Then silence on his part, as he listened to the response.

"No, I don't think that's a good idea."

Both parents continued with their individual phone calls for several minutes. Finally, the cry of "Mommy, Mommy" came forth from the child. The mother glanced up from her mindless doling of toast pieces, but continued her conversation.

Apparently frustrated, the child threw his bottle. Noting this, the mother started to wrap up her phone call while retrieving the bottle and some pieces of toast from the floor. The father stood and walked out of the breakfast room and into an adjoining area, cell phone to ear.

The mother finally concluded her call and turned her full attention to her young son. "You are misbehaving this morning. That is *not* how good little boys behave at the breakfast table!"

No, but neither is it how good parents behave. This learned behavior of negative attention-getting apparently begins in the high chair.

This real story exemplifies the upcoming generation of young people raised on cell phones and connected by emails or text messages, with very little personal human interaction, except perhaps, *with their teachers*. On a regular basis, one can witness young people of every age seemingly "attached" to their cell phones. If they aren't talking, they are "texting." Far more serious is the problem of *"sex-ting,"* the sending of outrageous sexual photos and messages. Teens spend an average of 11 hours a week online and send an average of 1742 text messages per month.[8]

According to Regina Lewis, an internet trend expert, some things about adolescents haven't changed—they participate in risky behaviors, and they do not consider the consequences or repercussions of those behaviors. There are physiological reasons for both of these phenomena. Their newfound hormones, high amounts of adrenalin, and the natural compulsivity of adolescents make high-risk behaviors *exciting*. And, the frontal lobe of the brain that warns of consequences does not fully develop until age 22 to 23.[9]

What *has* changed is how technology emboldens teens to take even greater risks than in the past. They can be *anonymous* on the Internet. They don't see the faces of the people who are reading their messages or viewing their pictures. Many are connected with social-networking sites such as Facebook and Twitter. With all of this, a new "language" for online use has been generated: pa = parent alert, pos = parent over shoulder, tdtm = talk dirty to me, iwu = I want you. Some of this "language" borders on profanity by any adult standard, which is always prohibited by school behavior codes. Young people have an easy way to say, do, or even to purchase things online that they would never consider in a face-to-face interaction. And there is no age limit on these sites, except that imposed by savvy and informed parents.

In all of this "anonymous" interaction, youngsters fail to realize that potential colleges and employers have access to these sites, as well. A seemingly innocent video on You-tube at age 12 may come back to haunt them at age 18 or 24 when they apply for college entrance, a scholarship, or a new job.

When they aren't on their phones, youngsters are in front of their computers or their television sets. Infants watch *Baby Einstein*. Preschoolers are placed in front of televisions as techno-baby-sitters. Programs are lively and full of action and fun . . . and often, violence. Problems are resolved in 30-minute segments. A 15-year-old today has not known a life that did not have computers in the classrooms and in the home.

The American Academy of Pediatrics warns of the dangers of the radiant light emitting from the "box screens" of TV and computers for all children under the age of two. Studies have shown this type of light to stunt neural growth. Another study reported in *Archives of Pediatrics and Adolescent Medicine,* July 2005, found "excessive television viewing in childhood may have long-lasting adverse consequences for educational achievement and subsequent socioeconomic status and well-being."[10]

Researchers have further concerns regarding the proximity of cell phone "waves" near human brains for extended periods. Several studies have shown that cell phones affect alpha brain waves—the attention or "mind wandering" waves. This effect continues long after the phones have been shut off, and are known to negatively affect sleep patterns of the users. The distance from the brain and the duration and frequency of use increases the impact. Studies are underway to determine possible causal effects of brain cancers related to cell phone use.

Considering the amount of time spent by young people on their cell phones, and the radio frequencies emitting from all kinds of electronic devices in their world, one can only imagine the horrific possibilities for *developing* brains.

Technology and Social-Emotional Development

Putting all physical harm aside, what is all of this technology doing for the social-emotional development of our young people? In many homes, the television is on during mealtimes. Conversations are infrequent and lack depth or serious content. Human interactions are rare. Do our young people know how to look someone in the eye when speaking to them? Can they produce a firm handshake when meeting someone? Do they know, and use, the words "please," "thank you," and "you're welcome?" Do they hold open a door for someone with an armload of books? Do they know how to carry on a simple conversation? Do they know how to listen? Do they know how to extend, or receive, a compliment? Do they know how to ask for something, face-to-face? Do they know how to resolve a conflict? In essence, do they know how to interact with other human beings?

Furthermore, have they considered the implications of sex-ting or of the real dangers of some of their Internet interactions? Most likely, these kinds of cautions will come from their teachers, who should be trained and informed about Internet safety.

The fact is, **students will spend far more time, and have infinitely more human interaction with their teachers than with anyone else.** For that reason alone, this new *R* called *Relationship* is critical for education in the twenty-first century. It is also crucial for any quality learning to occur in the classroom.

Take five minutes to do the following activity with a colleague:

- Sit in a chair facing each other. Label one as person *A* and the other as person *B.*
- Person *B* is to maintain eye contact with person *A.*
- Person *B* is to slightly lean toward *A*, nod affirmatively and avoid speaking while *A* has one minute to tell *B* about the most positive, influential teacher in her/his life.
- Person *A* then switches roles with *B,* and *B* shares with *A* for one minute about the most positive, influential teacher in his/her life.

When the time is up for both *A* and *B*, make a list of things said by your partner about his/her teacher. How much of the list is comprised of items that helped build a quality *relationship* with the teacher? Additionally, take a moment to examine what you were *feeling* inside as you were sharing memories of this positive, influential teacher.

Now think about your students. What might their list about *you* look like? List some of *their* possible responses below:

_____

_____

_____

_____

_____

_____

_____

By doing this activity, one can see that what teachers have in their hearts is more important than what they have in their heads.

Educators are always in *relationship* with students and can't take themselves out of the relationship. It will either be positive or negative, no in-between. Teachers must believe that they have the ability and opportunity to help students to be successful. It is imperative that they also believe that building quality relationships improves the attitude of both teacher and students. With this change in attitude comes a change in classroom behavior and increased academic success.

The Top Priorities of Schools have Changed

Education has become a business, and money is the driving force. It is a tough time to be a teacher.

The "No Child Left Behind" Act attaches tax dollars to test scores and threatens the loss of jobs for teachers whose classes do not perform well. Top-notch, innovative educators are being pushed to "teach to tests," and to deal with students as *products*—human capital, or merely potential workers in the near future.[11] Often, a single, *right answer* is expected on these tests, thereby stifling creativity and joyful learning.

Add to this an economy that is in a crisis paralleling that of the Great Depression. Already tight school budgets are experiencing further slashing. More jobs are threatened. The school climate is tense. The *business* is in jeopardy.

For many, fear abounds, and avoidance flourishes. We've all heard these words in the teacher break rooms:

- I'm too busy already. I don't have time to focus on relationship.
- Eventually, this will all go away.
- It really isn't that bad.
- It's not my problem. I'm just paid to teach math (or English, or . . .)
- I'm not sure what to do.

All of these excuses are just that—excuses!

Building quality *relationships* between staff and students is crucial for a successful education system today. It takes effort and time, but it is vitally important for educators do so, and it pays off in great rewards in the end. The real stories and practical tools in this book are designed to help instructors build **Relationship** with their students . . . to begin the journey to effective education in the twenty-first century.

No printed word no spoken plea
Can teach young minds
What they should be.
Nor all the books
On the shelves
But what teachers are themselves.
—Rudyard Kipling

The importance of building quality relationships with students is obvious. For many students, it is far more important than the subject taught, as evidenced in the following story:

Real Stories: A Christmas Treat

A few years ago Dave was Christmas shopping at a local mall when he heard a voice cry out, "Mr. O., Mr. O." Looking around he located a young man running through the crowd of shoppers toward him. Approaching Dave he asked, "Do you remember me?" Sadly, Dave shook his head. The young man informed him that he had been a student of his in a seventh-grade science class twelve years ago. He re-introduced himself by saying, "I don't remember much of what you taught me about science, but I do remember how you treated me." He put Dave in a giant bear hug and said, "It's great to see you. Merry Christmas!"

Our students may not remember a larger portion of the content we teach them, but they remember how we treat them.

The following list and accompanying stories will examine some ways to build relationships with students:

- **Let your students see you as a person, not only a teacher.**
  When students see that you have thoughts, feelings, and interests similar to theirs, they can more easily make the "human connection," which is a critical factor in building quality relationships.

Real Stories: Being Authentic

Anna's health class had been discussing the grieving process. During this series of lessons, she lost a dear five-year-old friend in a tragic car accident. When she started to cry as she shared her feelings, the students looked positively stricken to see her showing this emotion.

Feeling guilty that perhaps she had shared too much, the next day she had her students anonymously respond to a few questions about the situation:

- "Should I have stuffed my feelings inside and not allowed myself to cry during the discussion?" (She was always telling them that tears are normal and healthy and help to heal, but being raised with three brothers, she had *never* allowed herself to cry.)
- "When I felt the tears coming, should I have stepped outside the room?"
- "Should I have told one of my students of Mac's death, and then left the room briefly to allow that student to share the story of my grief?"
- "Would you have preferred that I had stayed home until all of my crying was done?

Anna was so moved by their anonymous and beautiful responses that she kept them and still has them today.

- "Adults never give us a chance to care."
- "Adults tell us it's OK to cry, but they never **do** it."
- "You have always been here for *us*, now we can be here for *you*."
- "I was uncomfortable when you started crying, but it's OK that you did it—just don't do it too often!"

Anna learned a critical lesson. Although the students honestly communicated how important it was for her to be "real" with them it did *not* mean that they needed to know all of the gritty details of her life, nor would she be free to openly cry at every broken fingernail. But, when her mother was dying of cancer, she felt she could truthfully tell them that it was a difficult time and ask for their cooperation. Or, when menopause triggered some severe insomnia, she could tell them, "I didn't sleep for beans last night. This would *not* be a good day to mess with me!" Or, when she had a tumor and was facing some immediate surgery the next day, she made it a point to go to school to personally, and somewhat tearfully, share her fears with her students. Then she felt justified with a simple request: "Please behave for the sub! I need to deal with survival and not worry about whether you are behaving."

Following the surgery, one of her most troublesome students regularly visited her at the hospital to report on the "good behavior" of some of the wildest students in class.

Anna's *real* emotions and *real* requests generated some amazing behaviors from her students, allowing them to be real, as well.

Some educators may feel that Anna shared too much with her students, or that she should have remained private and aloof. For Anna, however, the moment was accidental and the lesson was for her benefit: being authentic allows teachers to connect with students in a much deeper way.

- *See students as people, not just students.*
  Educators need to become a part of their students' world beyond the classroom. It is important that students know that teachers care about them, long before they will care about any lesson. When teachers attend student activities, they are able to see students in a different light, and to appreciate talents that students may have beyond what is exhibited in the classroom.

"When students know that you care, they care about what you know."

- *Look for alternatives to detention.*
  Although classroom discipline is important, many times a student who is acting out is merely crying for attention. Having the student help set up a science lab or make a bulletin board may be a way to give the student the attention he/she needs while also providing an opportunity to build a positive relationship.

Real Stories: Getting Attention

Teaching in the foods lab allowed Anna to offer a unique kind of detention—Dirty Oven Detail (D.O.D.). Misbehaving students were expected to clean an oven—the old-fashioned scrubbing way, without any kind of oven cleaner. This punishment wasn't used often, but was held as a promise-threat for the most offensive, repeated behaviors.

Jake* was a perfect example of a student who merely craved attention. But, as a relatively new teacher, Anna was stymied as to how to give him positive, appropriate acknowledgment following Jake's fourth D.O.D. in less than two weeks. She was totally at a loss in determining how to turn around his cycle of misbehavior.

In a moment of desperation, she sat him down (privately, of course), and simply said, "Jake, if you want my attention . . . if you want to spend time helping me after school, or just hanging out, talking . . . you don't have to get in trouble to do so. I'm here everyday. You can just come in after school to visit, or to talk, without getting in trouble in class first."

Jake didn't become a model student following that conversation. But, he did rein in his misbehavior and rarely received D.O.D.s after that little chat.

*not his real name.

- *Respect goes both ways*.
  Put-downs don't work. When adults show respect to students, they usually will respond accordingly. Respect is more important than obedience. With respect, obedience will be exhibited for the right reasons and when appropriate. You will find more on respect in chapters 5 and 6.

- *Treat students with dignity and don't get involved in a battle of wills*.
  Educators must work to improve the students' attitudes. If attitude improves, so will behavior. Therefore, it is important to pick one's

battles wisely. Too many times students are backed into a corner and put on the defensive. As a result, power struggles develop that create *losers and losers*—when a student loses, the teacher also loses. Always deal with strong-willed students privately, never in front of their peers. And, sarcasm should never be a part of a teacher's strategy to change behavior. It only leads to a wedge in the teacher-student relationship and further destroys a chance for positive change. The teacher who says, "Let's talk about this problem as self-respecting individuals," gives the student a better chance for positive change. The teacher who is open to student feedback and puts students in a position for success will enhance their self-esteem and give them a true sense of dignity.

- *Maintain a positive attitude toward students and model the behavior expected from them.*
  Teachers who model appropriate behavior tend to have more success in modifying student behavior in positive directions. Those who don't tend to have many more behavioral and relationship problems with their students.

Real Stories: Self-Fulfilling Prophecy

Back in the 1960s, a middle-school teacher in Michigan studied the concept of "self-fulfilling prophecy"—what you look for and *expect* to happen will often occur, merely because you *looked* for it. When she caught herself thinking of one class of students as "monsters," she had to ask herself, "What am *I* doing to create their behavior?"

For the next several weeks, instead of eating lunch, she would visualize each of those students in a more positive way. She pictured each of them entering the classroom with a smile, delighted to be there, and her being delighted to see them.

Because she was now *looking* for good behavior instead of bad, the energy started to shift, and she began noticing improvements. Her students recognized a change in her attitude, and their attitude changed, as well. She now looks back at that class as one of her favorites.

- *Don't judge a book by its cover.*

  Sometimes, teachers think that they *know* their students. Perhaps students dress in a certain way, have body piercings, tattoos, or bright green hair. Maybe students are judged by the friends they have, or their character, or lack of it, or even by behavior exhibited by their parents. Or, it could be that they exude the body language of closed-mindedness or hostility. The longer one teaches, the more "convinced" he may become that he *knows his students*, without really knowing them at all!

Real Stories: The Phone Number

At the beginning of each new class, a teacher gave out her phone number and invited students to call her in any crisis. If she were to have to pick one student over the years with whom she felt little "connection," someone who she was *certain* just wasn't "getting it," she would have chosen Harold.*

Imagine her surprise when she received a phone call from him three years after having had him in class, indicating that he "had a friend with a problem." Certain that she *knew* the friend to be Harold himself, and that the *"problem"* would most likely be drug usage, she still played out the phone-call scenario and began looking for the phone numbers of addiction counselors.

When Harold reported that his friend was being raped by her father every night, the teacher, speechless, closed the phone book and began really listening. She had been so sure that Harold was the one with the problem . . . so sure that he didn't get any of the lessons from her class . . . so quick to judge. Yet, it was Harold who got the most important lesson of all—that he could come to her for help in a crisis, even if it was years after the class was over.

*not his real name.

- *Use practical discipline strategies.*

  When you must discipline, do so for correction, not retaliation. Never deliberately embarrass a student—it doesn't work, and it decreases the chances for the teacher to build a positive relationship with the student. For more on discipline and punishment, see chapter 6.

Remember, we are always in relationship with a student and we can't take ourselves out of that relationship. It will either be positive or negative. The teacher must believe that he/she has the ability and a better-than-average chance to help students succeed. It is imperative that teachers also believe that building quality relationships with students will enhance success.

The greatest single attribute of relationship-driven teachers is the willingness and ability to take an honest and non-defensive look at the effectiveness of their own behavior, especially how their behavior influences interactions that occur in the classroom.[12]
—John Vitto

Chapter 3 Thought Starters

1. Have you ever cried in front of your students, or really lost your temper, or shared something significant about your personal life? What was the short-term effect of your being authentic? Long term?

2. Is your existing discipline strategy more corrective or retaliatory? What will you do to make your strategy more effective in building positive relationships with your students?

3. Can you honestly say you know something personal (outside the classroom information) about each one of your students? If not, what will you do to change that?

4. Recollect your most memorable teachers, both good and bad. Make a list of the qualities or characteristics that they exhibited. What makes the good ones stand out? Subject matter? Age—young or old? Classroom discipline—strict or lenient? Their personal dress code—professional or casual? Sense of humor? Respect? Sarcasm?

Your favorite teachers

_____

_____

_____

Your least favorite teachers

_____

_____

_____

5. What is the common thread regarding the teachers you cared about the most? The least?

6. If your students were asked to compile a similar chart, where might they list you and why?

Chapter 4

Relationship Benefits for Teachers and for Students

If you want to be happy within your heart, do for others.
Being unwanted, unloved, uncared-for, forgotten by everybody,
I think that is a much greater hunger,
a much greater poverty
than the person who has nothing to eat.
—Mother Teresa

Educators are role models, heroes, and surrogate parents for every student in their classrooms. These roles may come with unexpected consequences and unexpected "paychecks."

Teachers are Heroes

Teachers seldom know the impact they may have on students at every age and stage of development. But, it should never be taken for granted that educators are impacting *every student* in either a positive or a negative way. And, they must be constantly vigilant of their words and actions in these critically important relationships.

Real Stories: The Letter

In the middle of her career, a high school writing teacher received a three-page, beautifully handwritten letter from a former student. Words of love and appreciation poured from the pages. This young woman described the details of her life at that time, how the teacher had made a tremendous impact on her then, and how that impact continued by creating a highly successful person today.

Sadly, when the teacher reached the signature, she did not remember this person whose life she had changed. Because this student had hidden her adolescent pain behind a mask of quiet shyness, she did not *stand out* in her memory as some of the "really good," or the "really bad" students did.

The letter became another important reminder for this teacher to touch every student every day.

Teachers are Surrogate Parents

When a student is in the classroom, by law, teachers are considered *in loco parentis*—Latin for "in place of a parent." All educators are legally bound to act in lieu of parents—to take on some of the functions and responsibilities of parents, and to act in the best interest of their students. This includes, but is not limited to, a mandated reporting of suspected child abuse or neglect.

Aside from any legal obligations, teachers often feel *connected* to many of their students as if they were their own children. They laugh with them in their joy, and sometimes cry with them in their sorrow. They feel the pain of a broken friendship, or a broken heart. They even feel a sense of *pride* at their accomplishments.

Real Stories: Bursting with Pride—Anna's story

Alex* had just run his first regional track meet as a sprinter. He had been one of my favorite athletes on my intermediate school track team, so I was attending this important high school meet to support his efforts and to celebrate his continued success.

Alex's mother happened to be standing next to me as he crossed the finish line in third place, thereby qualifying for the state championship meet. The incredible sense of joy and pride I felt was almost overwhelming, and I shared these strangely intense feelings with Alex's mom. I could only imagine what she must have been feeling at that moment.

Alex's mother smiled. "Yes, I'm also bursting with pride. But later on, I'll still have to pick up his dirty socks!"

*not his real name.

Surrogate Parenting can be a Touchy *Subject*

As surrogate parents, teachers are often put in the position where *the students* have a need to be hugged by the them.

This brings forth some very *touchy* questions:

- When is it okay for a teacher to hug a student?
- Does it make a difference if the teacher is a male or a female?
- Does it make a difference if the student is male or female?
- Does the age of the student make a difference? Kindergartner? Senior?
- Does the *age of the teacher* make a difference? Age 25 or 65?
- Should the teacher ask permission first, even if he/she strongly feels that the student has a *need* to be hugged?
- Does it make a difference if it's a spontaneous moment on a playing field, or a saddened moment in the confines of one's classroom?

- Does the teacher's standing in the educational community make a difference?
- Does the community in which one teaches make a difference?
- Are there any written rules in the school district regarding appropriate and inappropriate touch?

Real Stories:
High Fives, Handshakes, and a Whole Lot of Hugs

While attending a Character Education Conference one summer, Dave met Hal Urban, a successful classroom teacher for thirty-five years. In Hal's presentation titled "Positive Words, Powerful Results," he described a daily greeting ritual he had with his students. As they entered, students had to give him a handshake, high five, or a hug before they were allowed into class.

Initially, Dave thought this practice was a bit "over the top." Little did he know of the powerful impact this "ritual" would have in the upcoming school year—the most challenging academic venture of his teaching experience.

In the fall of 2004, his at-risk coordinator duties expanded to include teaching one section of seventh grade science to a full class of thirty-six students, many of whom had a history of academic failure and behavior issues. Four of these students were diagnosed with ADHD, and after the very first class period, Dave knew he faced a formidable challenge.

Although he used various process-centered methods of instruction to meet this demanding situation, he decided to also try Hal Urban's "high five, handshake or hug policy" with students as they started their day. Dave added the knuckle rub (two people making a fist and touching the hand knuckles together), as that is what he saw students doing in the hallways. He announced the new policy, explaining that if they chose the hug, he would give them a *side hug* to prevent any suspicions of inappropriate touching.

Dave expected sarcastic remarks and much opposition to this new daily routine. To his complete surprise, he detected none of this. The first couple of weeks, he got mostly knuckle rubs and handshakes

---

with little eye contact. As time went on, eye contact improved, as did the classroom atmosphere. Tardiness became rare as students made it a priority to arrive on time for their greeting. Within a few months, a remarkable transition had occurred—*most of the students, including the boys, were lining up outside the classroom before class, waiting for their hugs.* The teacher across the hall from his room commented, "This is really no joke. The kids really *want* the hugs." Dave's response was, "No. They really *need* the hugs."

Although there were days when Dave had his doubts and troubles, teaching these challenging students was one of the most personally rewarding experiences in his K-12 career. One of the greatest lessons he learned was this: *"It is not about what is wrong with them, but about what I, as the classroom teacher, am going to do about it."*

Being a *high-tech and low-touch society* is taking its toll on our youngsters' self-worth. Dave's challenging students taught him many valuable life lessons, including the fact that people *need* to be *appropriately* touched.

Teachers are Role Models

Whether a teacher is subconsciously the surrogate parent, or merely the teacher at the front of the room, he/she is constantly and evermore a **role model** for students. And, those youngsters will be the harshest critics when educators fail in this role. Therefore:

- If you want students to be honest, you must first be honest with them. Don't tell youngsters one thing and then act in a different way. Don't have "trick questions" on tests or threaten consequences that will never be enforced. Students need to learn that they can trust teachers at their word.
- Discuss the issue of cheating with students, and establish severe consequences for breaking that rule. (See Anna's story about cheating in chapter 5.)
- If you want your students to be respectful, model respect. Be polite to them. Expect and insist on this behavior from them at all

times. Say "please," and "thank you," and insist that they use those courtesies in your classroom. Have appropriate consequences for failure to show respect to you and others. Apologize when you forget to be respectful.

- If you want your students to be prompt, model promptness. Start and finish class "on the minute." Provide classroom routines, such as "warm ups" or other class starters, where students become quiet and immediately begin working at the bell. Begin and conclude your lessons on time.
- If you want students to turn in their work on time, make sure that you return graded papers in a timely and promised manner. Have consequences for late work, and make sure the consequences mean an *inconvenience for the student*. Reducing their grades often means very little to many students. However, requiring that the student come in every day after school until the task is done correctly will send a message that you *want* them to succeed, and you'll be there every day until they do.
- If you think flexibility is an important character trait, model it for your students. For example, allow a grace period for a one-time late assignment. Or, provide extra credit opportunities for that time when they may have felt ill during a major test, or may have had an emotional crisis the night before. In other words, allow them the right to be human by the way you respond with flexibility to real-life teen situations.

Whether educators want to admit it or not, their students *do* look up to them as role models. For many students, teachers are the only positive models in their lives. No one expects a teacher to be a saint, but one ought to be ready to practice what one preaches, not just in the classroom, but also in the community in which he or she lives. It is unacceptable to get drunk at the local bar on Saturday night, and then lecture students about the evils of alcohol on Monday morning.

Part of developing honest relationships with students requires teachers being genuine in who they are. Young people are geniuses at spotting a fake—and exhibiting this kind of dishonesty is unforgivable to them.

On the other hand, it is equally unwise to share too much of one's personal lifestyle with students. A good general rule is: your personal life, and theirs, should remain just that—personal.

Teachers Touch the Lives of Students

Educators never fully know the lives that they touch. A single sarcastic or critical comment could cause a lifetime scar. Or, a simple classroom routine or coaching rule or expectation could create a leap of faith for someone—a boost of confidence that might carry them to a successful life.

The power teachers hold to influence the lives of the children entrusted to them is enormous. Often they never know of it, or may temporarily forget what they do know.

Real Stories: Creativity Shutdown

When Anna was in the sixth grade, Mrs. Popsicle* told her that she had "the creativity of a cow." Since Anna was a must-please-the-teacher kind of kid, Mrs. Popsicle was probably trying to motivate her to do her own thing, rather than satisfy the teacher's wishes. However, it backfired—for the next forty years, Anna collected art supplies for a class that she would take *someday* . . .

Someday did not come until her retirement. Within a few short weeks, she had created watercolor paintings that were featured in student art shows and now hang on her walls. All of those years were wasted because of a single thoughtless comment by one teacher.

*not her real name.

Consequences for Breaking the Connection

Sometimes, good intentions can backfire and break the teacher-student connection. Educators need to take care in dealing with *all* students.

Real Stories: The Evaluation

At the end of every semester class, Anna asked her students to evaluate the class structure and content, as well as her teaching style. During one such evaluation, she happened to notice that a group of her favorite, top-notch, all-A students had bright colored pens, and she was particularly eager to read the colored responses of her brightest and best.

Imagine Anna's shock to find all of their ratings as 5s, the lowest possible, and all of their comments were as negative as any she had *ever* received!

What had happened? How could she be perceived so negatively by that entire group of top-notch students? Typically, she received quite good evaluations from her students, with only a rare negative comment or two.

In looking back, she realized that she had spent an extensive amount of time working with a very troubled girl named Darla.* In Anna's mind, she knew that Darla *needed* the additional attention and effort, and that the all-A table got attention with their perfect grades and perfect classroom behavior.

While Darla's behavior improved dramatically under Anna's loving concern, she had lost the respect of six others in that class, and potentially every other student who also needed her attention and acknowledgment.

From that day forward, Anna made it a point to make contact with *every* student, *every* day. It may have been a greeting at the door, a farewell as they left, or a personal comment about their basketball game the previous night. Even if only taking a few seconds of her time, these daily moments of connection made a difference, because for many, it was the only personal attention they received.

*not her real name.

Anyone who has been in education for a while could share stories similar to the ones you have read thus far. Like parenting, no one is perfect in teaching. But good educators will have a passion for their job. It is not uncommon for those who care to quickly realize the benefits of a strong teacher-student bond. For some, however, this awareness may not come until years later, in the form of college graduation invitations, wedding announcements, and baby pictures. If you're lucky, you'll receive a letter of gratitude from an almost-forgotten student. If you're *really* fortunate, you'll have on-going photos, emails, and Christmas cards from students that you had over thirty years ago. Whatever the form, it will give pause for a moment of reflection and a smile.

Cherish these moments, for they are the *real paychecks* of teaching!

Good Teachers Pass on Their Inspiration

Today's teachers learned from other teachers who made a connection with them—with their heart, soul, and personal spirit of education. They may even have learned some positive classroom techniques that they ended up using with their own students.

Real Stories: Passing the Baton

Mrs. Stamm was a role model for Anna in high school. She was nice, and fun, and encouraging, and she made Anna feel competent and valued. Anna became a teacher because she wanted to be just like Mrs. Stamm someday.

Coach Osburn was a role model for Anna when she was a new teacher. He was respected and liked by *everyone* who knew him—the jocks, the burnouts, the nerds, the school leaders, the "challenged" students, the intellectuals, the teachers, the administrators, and the community. Anna wanted to be a teacher just like him someday.

Anna was a role model for Jessica,* a very shy girl in the seventh grade, who blossomed because of an assignment called "warm fuzzies." Jessica is now teaching in a major city and had her fourth graders write Anna letters of appreciation for being a positive role model for their favorite teacher.

Anna was a role model for Eric,* a former Marine, turned middle-school teacher. He fondly remembers his most difficult workouts on the track team—an important reminder that he *can* do the tough stuff, and to believe in himself.

And so it continues . . .

*not their real names.

Today's educators must pass on that baton. They must connect in ways that challenge other young people to *want* to inspire, to motivate, to teach, and to make the world a better place . . . one student at a time.

The Real Benefits *of Relationship*

The previous section focuses on the benefits for the *teachers*—but what about the *students?* What are the advantages for them in developing quality relationships with each of their teachers?

The answer to that can best be summed up with the following:

> Better behavior
> Better behavior
> Better behavior
> Greater success
> Greater success
> Greater success

Simply said, **students will learn more from the teachers with whom they have a positive connection.**

Success, Success, Success

In the classroom or on the playing field, helping students to reach success is a beautiful thing.

Real Stories: One Moment in Time

Dave was an athletic coach for twenty-five years, and one of the sports he coached was high school varsity football.

In the fall of 1991, he was in his sixth year as an offensive coordinator for the Saginaw Arthur Hill Lumberjacks' football team. Over the years, the team made good runs in the state playoffs but never made it to "the big dance," the state championship game in the Pontiac Silverdome.

The coaching staff viewed that season as one of rebuilding. All the stars had graduated and the 1991 team was void of any high-caliber players. They were small, slow, and lacked the athleticism found in previous years. The only team goal for the year was a realistic one: "Let's get better." The coaching staff felt that they were going to have to be magicians to make it through the regular season; qualifying for the state playoffs wasn't even a consideration.

The team was composed of a unique group of young men who truly cared for one another and their coaching staff, and worked harder and showed more respect than any previous team. They may have been low on talent, but they were high on character, and were one of the most enjoyable teams ever coached by that staff. They sincerely cared for each other, their families, their school, and their community.

They started the season by winning three of their first five games. The coaching staff secretly felt that if they could possibly win two more games, they would consider the season a success. The last four games of the season turned out to be nerve-racking nail-biters, but they won them all. Finishing in second place in the conference, they *qualified for the playoffs!*

The first playoff game was against the conference champions. Scoring a touchdown with no time remaining in the game to tie the score, they won the game in an exciting overtime period. No one outside of the team had given them a chance, but the coaches had learned to believe in this special group of young men.

The second playoff game was against the number one ranked AA team in the state—a team with a history rich in success in the state of Michigan. Traveling 150 miles and playing them on their home field in front of 12,000 fans, the team was once again picked for a big loss. Winning 21-18, it seemed like the whole sports world of Michigan was in shock.

The following week they were underdogs once again. Winning with a final score of 29-0, they were headed to "the big dance" to play another state powerhouse with a winning tradition.

At a team meeting to start out the week of preparation for the game, the players made a vow to remain positive no matter what the news media was saying about their chances of winning. They also vowed that no matter what the outcome of the game, they would hold their heads high and never lose the respect that they had for each other. Once again as huge underdogs, they were predicted to lose by three or four touchdowns.

In this final, championship game, they scored a touchdown with one minute and fifteen seconds left in the game to win 13-12. They were Class AA state champions! The headlines in the Saginaw News the next morning read, *"Unbelievable."*

Overcoming the Odds

Why did this group of young men accomplish more than the highly talented teams that came before them? The coaches believe the answer is found in the **relationships** that the players had. The players were more open to being taught, took correction without affront, and gave their best effort. They *believed* that they could be more than anyone thought they could be.

The same is true in academia. The learning atmosphere of the classroom is enhanced when quality relationships exist between student and teacher, and between students and their classmates. Students who are more excited to learn are more open to correction, behave better, make stronger efforts, and enjoy the journey and joy of education.

The football team probably also had some luck along the way. But the key to this wonderful learning experience was the *quality relationships* that existed on the team. Those relationships were taught and modeled by adults, including parents, teachers, and coaches. The relationship lessons provided them with an opportunity to experience success in whatever endeavors they were to pursue.

Who Else Benefited?

The success of these young men was also beneficial to the entire student body, staff, and surrounding community. Their accomplishments laid the foundation for success in other areas of the school environment and gave younger students a good example to follow. It wasn't the talent, it was the *heart* of the players that enabled them to achieve the state's highest honor in high school football, and it gave each of them a blueprint for success in life.

It Is What One Believes . . .

It is very important for educators to closely examine their beliefs and the reasons behind those beliefs. In conversations with students, they believe *the best teachers **care** the most, not **know** the most.* If one believes that developing quality relationships with students will result in quality education, then actions and behavior need to reflect this belief. Once reflected, educators must also believe that their students will be better people for having had them as a teacher. It is the examination of one's belief system that makes the difference and influences the building of and the benefits of quality relationships.

Real Stories: I Hate Math!

In a small, rural high school in the 1960s, every math class was taught by the same teacher—Mr. Sterling. He was a good teacher, and was also the sponsor for the *Future Teachers' Association* (F.T.A.). Mr. Sterling was a gentle man whose daughter and sons attended the school, and he loved to sing. Many times, he led the singing of Christmas carols at the F.T.A. meetings.

His students *liked* him—a lot—because it was obvious that he really *cared* about them. Even the students who hated math *wanted to care* about math because of him. When they would get frustrated and want to quit, especially on those dreaded story problems, they would not give up because they didn't want to disappoint Mr. Sterling.

Mr. Sterling's students may have never grown to love math, but they certainly *learned* math—many scoring the highest in the state on the math section of every major standardized test they took.

Behavior, Behavior, Behavior

Most teachers' worst nightmare will be their disruptive students, but these students *can* become the teacher's greatest ally.

Real Stories: War Stories in the Teacher's Lounge

A new educator entering the district mid-year, soon heard about Connor*—the "most evil student in the entire school," or so it seemed to some of the veteran teachers. One teacher would tell a tale of Connor's misbehavior, only to be "topped" by another, *"If you think **that** is bad, you should hear what he did in **my** class . . . "*

Not wanting to enter in to this teacher-lounge gossip, this newbie made it her personal mission to win Connor over to her side. Connor turned out to have a *very* large "chip" on his shoulder and an extremely rare, but brilliant smile. Unfortunately, his behavior matched his "chip." Remembering the "self-fulfilling prophecy" (that

---

which you seek, you shall find), the teacher chose to ignore Connor's underlying anger, creating situations where she might encounter the *real Connor* that she knew to be there.

Every day, she flashed Connor her most wonderful smile and offered him a cheerful greeting, expecting nothing in return. When his misbehavior demanded her attention, she was careful to *clearly* separate the behavior from the person.

She began to delegate important tasks to Connor and to compliment him on his football game or his class work. She sent a *positive* note to his parents following one of Connor's good days. Later, at a Parent Open House, his parents tearfully shared that they had *never* received any positive correspondence from the schools in all of the years that Connor had attended in the district. They taped her note to the refrigerator door.

Little by little, the teacher made a concerted effort to whittle away at Connor's "chip." From the very first day, *her* experience with Connor was nothing like the war stories in the teacher's lounge. Her genuine concern for this young man ultimately changed his classroom behavior. And what started out as a personal challenge to get Connor to behave, blossomed into a teacher-student connection that lasted for many years.

*Connor is not his real name.

Look for Loveable and Capable

An educational speaker once said that with all students who misbehave, you should look for a large, but invisible W imprinted on their foreheads—the W stands for wounded.

Students never enter classrooms as evil persons. They don't *want* to fail, nor do they *want* to be disliked or to cause trouble. Some of them simply come to school as *wounded,* and one of the tasks of teachers is to help heal the wounds that interfere with their academic and social successes. The best way, and sometimes the only way to do that is to create positive *relationships* with them.

What Educational Experts Believe

One does not have to research the educational literature for very long to discover comments by respected educators concerning benefits of teacher-student relationship building. The following is a short version of what can be an extremely long list:

"80% of students entering school feel good about themselves. By the end of the fifth grade only 20% do. Only one in five high school students has positive self-esteem." **National Assessment of Education Progress, National Parent Teacher Association**[1]

"The quality of teacher-student relationships is the keystone for all other aspects of classroom management." **Morzano & Morzano,** *Dimensions of Learning,* **Morzano Research Library, 2007.**[2]

"A strong relationship with a caring adult enables at-risk youth to make life altering changes." **Werner & Smith,** *Overcoming the Odds: High Risk Children from Birth to Adulthood,* **Cornell University, 1992**[3]

"Research shows that having positive and caring relationships in schools increases resilience and protects children from academic failure, mental illness, alcohol and drug abuse, and destructive behavior and violence." **Resnick, et al., 1997**[4]

"Most long term psychological problems are the result of problems in one or more significant relationships in a person's life. Therefore, when teachers create a positive and personal relationship with students, they may be preventing the development of psychological problems in their students." **William Glasser,** *Choice Theory: A New Psychology of Personal Freedom,* **Harper-Collins, 1998.**[5]

There is no need to expound on the above statements, as they stand on their own.

Building Bonding

Every good teacher uses a variety of techniques to create feelings of safety within his/her classroom and to promote bonding with students. From games and gimmicks, to journal writing assignments, to cartoons and quotes, to graffiti walls and stuffed animals, to hugs and high-five greetings at the door, to the use of stories; each day offers new opportunities to make connections with every student.

Based on her classroom experience with the power of story to foster student bonding, Anna offers the following recommendations:

Five Things You Can Do To Foster Student Bonding in Your Classrooms

Creating an emotionally honest and safe learning environment may not be easy, but here are a few simple suggestions:

1. **Create a climate where students feel safe to experience a wide range of feelings**. They cannot express joy without also accessing their sorrow, anger, or frustration. In addition, they must learn how to communicate these feelings in appropriate ways. Ultimately, this empowers them to cope with life.

2. **Read to students at *every level, every day***. My college students enjoy hearing a good story as much as my younger students did. Stories make heart-to-heart connections: student-to-self, student-to-student, and student-to-teacher. Stories provide a quick access to feelings, and follow-up writing is a good way to express these emotions.

3. **Research shows that successful people read**. You need not be an English teacher to model reading for your students. I know math, Spanish, and science teachers who regularly read to their students. You can read short, motivational stories, or pages from a book that relates to your subject matter—perhaps a book on Nikola Tesla, President Obama, or anyone who captures your passion, for it is your passion that will shine through and connect with your students.

---

4. **Choose stories that present the messages that you desire**—stories of hope, determination, overcoming obstacles—true stories of personal empowerment. For me, the daily dose of Chicken Soup significantly and positively changed classroom behavior. Lost time spent reading more than compensated for less time spent disciplining.

5. **Practice random acts of kindness**, and create classroom projects where students can experience the joyfulness of giving, and where they recognize their connection with, and responsibility toward, others on this planet.*

* originally published in *YES Magazine*, January, 2009.[6]

Finding Your Relationship Path

The story examples presented in this chapter are not intended to determine the best way for you to make connections with your students. *Real Stories* are simply that: real stories. They may have worked for the authors of this book and others, but times were different then, just as the authors are different from each other, and they are from each of you. Anna, as a female teacher in her fifties had a different kind of connection with students than Dave did when he was twenty-five.

The primary message is to first teach children. The curriculum and content will automatically follow. Build relationships first, and the subject matter will flow from having made those connections.

Distance learning and on-line classes can never replace a joyful, enthusiastic, creative teacher at the front of the room. Learning from a TV or computer "box" can never generate the excitement that a good teacher can create. Nor should anyone attempt to replace teachers with television screens under the guise of "balancing the budget."

The future of the entire world depends on society's investment in educating the children—their most important commodity. Until such time as that investment is a financial one, it must be an emotional one on the part of every teacher with every student in every classroom in every school. For it is that relationship with students that will inspire their love of learning—and that will light a fire for them to change the world.

Students care about what you know, only when they
know that you care!

Chapter 4 Thought Starters

1. Take five minutes to recall significant students and the lessons that *you learned from them*.

Student/Lesson

_____

_____

_____

_____

_____

_____

2. Take a few minutes to write your *"mental rules"* for hugging students. How do you stand on this *"touchy"* issue?

_____

_____

_____

_____

_____

_____

It helps to have thought about this issue **before** you are faced with it. As a parent, a hug is a normal behavior, often expected in certain circumstances. What are the rules for you as *surrogate parent* for hugging your students?

3. What are some of *your* core beliefs about teacher-student relationships? Take five minutes to list some of them below.

_____

_____

_____

_____

_____

_____

4. What qualities do you possess that would cause your students to look up to you? List some of them here:

_____

_____

_____

_____

_____

_____

Part Three

Respect

Chapter 5

Three Cornerstones of Respect

A Brief History of Respect in the Classroom

Prior to the 1960s, showing respect for the teacher was absolute and automatic, although the teacher need not show a similar behavior toward students. Any act of disrespect was severely dealt with by the teacher, and again by the parents when reported to the home. Neither parent nor student seriously questioned who was "right"—it was *always* the teacher.

Within the classrooms of the 1800s, language reflected respect—swearing was almost non-existent for males and totally inappropriate for females. Use of words like *damn, hell,* or *shit* would be cause for washing out one's mouth with soap—lye soap! Unlike today, where *the f-word* is a commonly heard adjective, in our early classrooms it was not even known to exist. On another note, manners were expected—*please, thank you, you're welcome, excuse me, pardon me, I'm sorry*—were common and expected courtesies.

Respect between students held a different quality then. There have always been bullies and children who insult verbally or physically harm other students, but it seems to have been less cruel, less constant, and less intense in the schools of the 1800s and early 1900s. And, it was rarely exhibited in the younger children. Certainly, students were not driven to die by suicide as a result of bullying, as is the growing and horribly frightening trend today.

Another aspect of respect is the issue of cheating, which is essentially a lack of self-respect. Rarely found in younger children, it was considered shameful at any age to be caught in such a dishonest act in 19th century classrooms.

Respect in Classrooms Today

The **R** of *respect* is, as a general rule, not found in classrooms today until a relationship is formed between teacher and student. Starting in the latter half of the 20th century, most teachers had to *prove* themselves to students—to *earn* their respect. Sadly, in the 21st century American schools, many teachers are not getting any respect at all.

In a May 2007 study featured in **Teacher** magazine, researchers found that 34% of America's teachers have considered quitting because of the disrespect evident everywhere in our culture and foremost in our classrooms.[1]

In some schools, students wear t-shirts carrying messages of drug use, sexual innuendo, or simply hatred of those who may be different. Other clothing worn to class may be highly sexual or suggestive—a reflection of what youngsters see on TV and their desire to emulate television and movie heroes.

A typical high school dance may have a girl sandwiched between two males in a spooning position that strongly resembles having sex with one's clothing on, all the while gyrating to the latest music, which often contains violent or sexually abusive messages.

And, the most frightening thing of all is the number of young girls, ages 11, 12, or 13, who are performing acts of oral sex on male classmates "just to please." These are often youngsters anyone would consider to be "nice girls." They may be cheerleaders, student council presidents, or sopranos in the church choir. They hardly appear to be sexually active. In fact, they do not consider this as a sexual act since they cannot get pregnant.

To add insult to injury, often a teacher's attempt to correct or to guide students on any of the aforementioned situations is met with demands for "student rights" and/or threats of parents bringing forth lawsuits.

Most of the examples found in this book consist of success stories. But teachers are far from perfect, and the following story is about one teacher's "less than proud" moment.

Real Stories: The Threat—Sarah's* story

Ted* is the *only* student I had in 31 years of teaching public school that I simply *did not like*. He was crude, rude, lazy, and obnoxious. Furthermore, he reminded me quite regularly of the fact that both of his parents were lawyers, and they would sue me if *he* didn't like what I did. And, he blatantly bad-mouthed anything to do with school. There was *nothing* that he wanted to learn! When he turned sixteen, his plan was to quit school and play drums in a rock band.

I pointed out that he might not be successful at that particular venture, and perhaps needed to *learn something* as a back-up plan. He scoffed at my suggestion and told everyone that he intended to use his parents' money to survive and to "lure chicks."

After the third day in a row of Ted threatening a lawsuit, I had had it. In front of the entire class, I turned to him and shouted, "*You can invite either or both of your parents to discuss a lawsuit with me at any time! In fact, I **welcome** the opportunity to discuss with them all of your complaints, as well as **my** concerns for your lack of work in here!*"

Not good role modeling on my part, but I had no intention of being threatened by Ted or his parents!

I've never admitted this before, but I could hardly wait for Ted to turn sixteen!

*Not their real names

Many teachers today face threats to their safety and their lives that go beyond the verbal threat in this story. Is it any wonder so many of America's teachers have considered quitting? Classroom discipline is at a standstill, seeming more like crowd control than education. Administrators are neck-deep in budget crises and often don't back teachers in enforcing disciplinary action. Parents, who used to be the teacher's number one ally, now fall into three categories of support, or lack of it:

1. Those who back their children and protect their child's "record" at any and all costs.
2. Those who throw their hands in the air while crying, "*I don't know what to do . . . .*"
3. Those rare parents who work *with* the schools to teach their children respect and responsibility (see chapters 7 and 8), as well as subject matter.

The common thread tying all of these stories together is a total lack of respect. The focus of this chapter will be on the three cornerstones of respect:

*   respect for self
*   respect for others
*   respect for property, the environment, the world

Respect for Self

> *Only by self-respect will you compel others to respect you.*
> —Fyodor Dostoyevsky

We've all heard, "It takes an entire village to raise a child." Perhaps this was never truer than with the topic of self-respect, and never more lacking than in today's world.

*   How do you teach someone to always put a best foot forward?
*   How do you teach someone to be clean of body, mind, and mouth?
*   How do you teach someone to value their body and to say *no* to all things that would harm it?
*   How do you teach someone to be a leader of good acts and ideas, rather than a follower of questionable ones?
*   How do you teach someone to honor commitments to oneself, be it time spent on homework, or keeping one's room clean?

- How do you teach someone that words have power, but you are only as good as the *actions* that follow?
- How do you teach someone that a person's name has honor?
- How do you teach someone to have pride in all that he or she does?

Ideally, all of these concepts would originate from the home. However, with many messages to the contrary being presented in the media, and a breakdown in the structure of the family, it falls to the schools to help instill and reinforce these basic values.

Although many youngsters are taught values in their religious institutions or receive character education in Scouts or other youth affiliations, in today's America, the school is still the central, socializing "village" that most children have. Part of the problem with schools teaching values is that no one can agree on what "Basic Values" are anymore. For this and other reasons, some parents pull their children out of public schools and put them either in private school or home-schooling co-ops where values are identified, stated clearly, taught, and upheld.

> *Respect your efforts, respect yourself.*
> *Self-respect leads to self-discipline.*
> *When you have both firmly under your belt, that's real power.*
> —Clint Eastwood

> *People seldom improve when they have no other model*
> *but themselves to copy.*
> —Oliver Goldsmith

Cheating Shows a Lack of Self-respect

Many of today's students consider cheating to be a normal, and sometimes "necessary" behavior, even in the elementary grades. This lack of self-respect is prevalent in American society and is a frightening trend in education.

Real Stories: Cheating

Anna provided many opportunities for success in her classes, and assured her students that there was no need to cheat to attain a good grade. After long discussions with her students about the importance of being honest, and her personal distaste for being a "test cop," she established two simple rules regarding cheating in her classes:

#1. If you cheat, you will likely be caught. It is just a matter of time.
#2. If you are caught, *you* will be *choosing* to accept the following consequences:

- First offense—you will tell your parents, and they will contact me to arrange a meeting to discuss your need or desire to cheat.
- Second offense—your parents will be expected to come to school to monitor *any* and *all* subsequent tests that you may take.

She did not have any second offenses.

Respect for Others

Perhaps the one area where it is most appropriate to *teach* respect is that of respect for others. Young people spend much more time in school with their teachers than they do at home with their parents. In addition, within the classroom, they are in a social setting that requires cooperation, tolerance, and basic manners in order for it to function smoothly.

Children *learn* fear, they *learn* hate, and they also *learn* respect. In a perfect world, families provide safe havens in which children grow and flourish at all levels. However, behind every troubled child is frequently a troubled parent-child relationship. In many cases, the education system is teaching *parents* how to engage with their children in ways where the child feels safe to express himself/herself and to share his/her pain. This skill set develops the inner strength that helps one to deal with outer criticism.

However, these feelings of acceptance, self-confidence, and safety are far from reality for many students and are a concern at every socioeconomic level. Children growing up in slum areas of our biggest cities are often caught between drug lords and gangs, and live in constant fear for their lives. Homicide is the number two killer of our teenagers today.[2] The poorest and most rural areas may have divorce, domestic violence, or perhaps even incest, and so do some of the richest and most prominent families. No one is immune from pain and suffering. These assaults on children are constant. The pressures wear on them over time, pushing many of them to attempt suicide in their teenage years. Approximately *fourteen adolescents a day* are known to have completed a suicide![3] Experts claim that one can take that number, and multiply it by 4.5 to get a more accurate number of daily accidental suicide deaths—deaths thought to be accidents, but in reality were completed suicides.

One thing is known: true learning does not take place in an environment of hostility and fear. It takes place only in safety and where respect is shown for everyone.

Teachers have the greatest opportunity to create this physical, emotional, and social safety zone. They begin by modeling respect at every juncture. Respect is a two-way street—you won't see it if you don't show it.

The A-B-C's of creating a classroom family

The following **A-B-C's** are critical in establishing a healthy classroom family:

A—**A**wareness of each other's similarities and differences.
B—**B**eing kind and respectful to each individual.
C—**C**onnecting with the group and feeling responsible for group outcomes.

As any educator knows, these A-B-C's are *simple,* but not *easy.*

A—Awareness of each other's similarities and differences:

It is important for you, as the teacher, to create experiences and situations that *bond* students into a single unit—a *family,* of sorts. Many of these activities seem like games to students, and are enjoyed by all age levels. For example:

- Use non-threatening ways to form partners or groups (hopping on one foot, finding someone with the same birth month, adding together your ages to come up with an even number, using a deck of playing cards to match students by number, etc.). The idea is to do it *quickly*, and in ways that no one feels that he/she is the "last one chosen." *Playfair* by Goodman and Weinstein is an older but highly recommended, wonderful book filled with these ideas.[4]

- Set up situations early in the year where students must interact with every other student in the class. Keep these activities short and sweet, so the sharing is not burdensome. Structure them so that students might find *similarities* with their classmates of which they were previously unaware.

- Set a tone for a healthy respect of differences, making those differences issues of curiosity and learning rather than criticism and judgment.

Real Stories: The Gimp

Beth,* a cheery ninth grader, walked with a pronounced limp. At age ten, Beth had to choose between an amputation or a cadaver transplant to deal with bone cancer in her leg. Formerly the fastest runner in her grade, it was the toughest choice of her life thus far. Choosing the amputation, she had a prosthesis made and therefore walked with a limp.

Knowing her full story, her teacher asked her if she would be willing to be the "resident expert" on the subject of cancer. Beth agreed.

Beth spoke to the class, sharing many stories of her journey with cancer—chemotherapy, losing her hair, and of losing two of her closest friends at Mott Children's Hospital—girls who had chosen the cadaver transplants and had died. She talked about drawing faces on the back of her bald head, the discomfort of wearing a prosthesis, and of the sadness of no longer being able to run. She talked about her fear of the cancer returning, and also of the "gift of cancer," which brought amazing people into her life.

Students who had known Beth for years were unaware of her as a cancer survivor, and some had been particularly cruel to her because of her limp. The day after her talk to the class, Beth received an apology letter from Tim,* the boy who had nicknamed her "Gimp" and who had tormented her for over four years! Beth and Tim went on to become good friends.

*not their real names

B—Being kind and respectful to each individual:

From the words we use, to the space we share, to the time that we spend together, it is important that we are respectful to all human beings, no matter what their station in life.

Words have power. Insist that students regularly use the words:

> Please
> Thank you
> You're welcome
> Pardon me
> I'm sorry
> Excuse me

Do not honor student requests that do not contain proper words of courtesy and respect. Negative words have power, too. Forbid the use of swear words, racial, religious, or ethnic slurs, homosexual bashing, gender put-downs, socioeconomic targeting, words discriminating against the physically or mentally challenged.

Also consider banning the words:

> I can't . . . I'll try . . .

"I can't" really means "I won't." For a wonderful story with related activities, read "Rest in Peace: The 'I Can't' Funeral," found in **Chicken Soup for the Soul in the Classroom**.[5]

On the other hand, "try" is actually a useless word. You either *do* something, or you *don't do* it. Trying is simply copping-out of *doing*—it is making an excuse for *not doing* something. (See *Appendix A* for a classroom demonstration of this concept.)

Here are some other ways students and teachers can demonstrate respect for each other:

- Respect time commitments with others.
  - Being on time
  - Starting on time
  - Ending on time
  - Turning in assignments on time
  - Returning classroom tests and papers on time
- Respect others' space.
  - Auditory (use of cell phones, loud music, slamming a door, etc.)
  - Olfactory (smoking, use of heavy colognes, personal cleanliness, etc.)
  - Kinesthetic (appropriate touch—a hug is OK, butt-grabbing is not)
  - Visual (wearing clothing that may be suggestive, offensive, or provocative)
- Honoring commitments
  - You are only as good as your word.
  - If you must break a commitment, communicate that, and re-negotiate.

> *As a leader, your word is only as good as your last promise*
> *kept . . . or broken.*
> —Barbara "BJ" Gallagher

C—Connecting with the group and feeling responsible for group outcomes:

At every juncture, teachers must provide students with the opportunity to understand the differences of others—to walk a mile in their shoes—to *connect* with them in some way that makes them feel a part of the group. You might want to investigate an amazing program for your school called *Challenge Day*. For more information, visit the website www. challengeday.org [6] Watch the video of activities designed to get students to really connect with each other. This program was featured on *Oprah* and is becoming famous nationwide.

After four suicides at a school in Hamilton, Ohio, they adapted Challenge Day, changed the name to Character Day, and spent hours and hours training a voluntary staff and student group in these methods as a way to get their students to accept each other throughout the school. Their story was featured on a PBS special entitled, "Cry for Help."[7]

With intense programs such as these, students don't fear coming to school. They know that when they go to school, everyone there is going to be nice to them and there is no reason to hurt oneself or others.

Unexpected Bonding Opportunities

Sometimes, lessons of respect or bonding opportunities may be accidental, as shown in the following story:

Real Stories: *Chicken Soup for the Soul*—Anna's Story

It was a teacher's nightmare—five minutes left in the class period, with a rowdy group of seventh graders. It was the first day back to school following a two-week Christmas break, and none of us was back in the classroom "groove" yet. As a veteran educator, I always over-planned my lessons by 15-20 minutes, but something had gone wrong that morning.

I looked at the clock, looked at my students, looked at the clock, and looked at my desk for anything that might magically fill the minutes. Sitting there was a Christmas present—*Chicken Soup for the Soul*. I grabbed it, randomly opened it to page 259 and began reading a true story of determination.

I finished the story moments before the dismissal bell, breathed a sigh of relief, and thought nothing more of the matter. The next day, several of my students walked into class requesting more of that "Chicken Soup thing..." I had read several of the stories at home and found them all to have wonderful messages of hope, determination, kindness, laughter, love, and life. Since each story took only two or three minutes to read, I felt it was not significantly taking time away from curriculum content. Plus, even my most disruptive students settled down for this story routine that ended each class period.

Thus began a classroom journey that had some very surprising side effects. In hindsight, I think it was what Jack Canfield calls "emotional literacy." Without realizing it, by reading these stories each day, I was creating a classroom environment where it was safe to access and express feelings. And, even more importantly, I was modeling this behavior for my students. If I read a sad story, I cried. At first, my students were mortified to see a teacher crying. Later, they would sometimes request a "cry story." With other stories, we might laugh so hard we would almost pee our pants!

Without ever talking about it, we were sharing our feelings on a daily basis, much as a family would do. And, slowly, we became a family. Each of my five classes developed its own unique classroom bond.

Weeks passed, and I saw that my students were treating each other more respectfully. Within months, I noticed changes in the hallways throughout the school. Following a story about a potential suicide, I saw students help to pick up dropped books, rather than to kick them down the hallway, laughing. The mother of a learning-disabled student almost ran me over in a parking lot. "What have you done to my daughter? She has never read a book in her life, and now she wants me to buy her this Chicken Soup thing. What is it?" Non-readers were becoming readers because they couldn't wait until the next day for a story.

I came to realize that my students were most *connected* when experiencing the full range of emotions that these stories brought forth. So, occasionally I would have them write about these feelings as classroom warm-ups. Sometimes I would choose longer stories, or make the story the focus of the lesson plan, rather than ending the class with this thought for the day. I didn't want this to become work for them or something to dread. It was important that my students welcome these stories, and, ultimately, the messages they contained. And, the frequency was crucial in creating the behavioral changes.

Understanding the power of this daily story process planted a seed for reaching more students. I approached Jack Canfield at a book signing to suggest that we co-author a book, *Chicken Soup for the Soul in the Classroom*—a book of stories, lesson plans, and activities for teachers. Exactly four years later, to the day, I had my first book signing in the same store. Together, we are now "changing the world, one student at a time, and one story at a time."

Dealing with Bullies and Disrespectful Behavior at Every Age

Throughout history, there have always been people who have used their physical or social power to intimidate or hurt others. In the Spring of 2009, there were several sad stories featured on the news or on television talk shows such as *Ellen* and *Oprah*—stories of children as young as 10 or 11 who completed suicide because of the escalating taunting behaviors in their schools.

Notice the use of the word, "completed," rather than "committed." Some survival-of-suicide groups have indicated that the use of "committed" is insensitive for the families who are left behind. People *commit* murder, bank robberies, and other crimes—their deceased loved one is not a criminal!

Obviously, the primary place where taunting, teasing, and bullying activity is most likely to occur is in the schools and their surrounding environs. Therefore, it falls to the teachers and coaches to be vigilant in seeking, monitoring, and then upholding the consequences for such behavior—not just at the elementary level—but throughout all the school years.

As reported on a PBS special, entitled "Cry for Help," school is a natural target for the alienated and violent kids, for it is the place where they perceive the most severe "wrongs" they have encountered in their lives. It offers them a means of "control" by deciding who will live and who will die. Add to that, the "copy-cat" effect, and it explains the increase in school shootings over the years.[8]

Most students will not report bullying situations for fear of even greater reprisals. It is the responsibility of every educator to learn the warning signs of potentially violent students, to watch for these behaviors and to protect *all* students.

An entire book could be written on this subject, but for the topic of *respect* in the context of the classroom, a few key questions and concepts will suffice:

- Shouldn't children of every age learn how to deal with their own problems, including bullies?

Yes, but educators are the perfect people to *teach* them. Remember that respect is a *learned* behavior. Teachers are on the fringes of student social interactions at all times, and in ways that parents never will be. In educating for all of society, this arena of social interaction is a critical one.

- Where will I fit this on my already over-filled platter?

If something is important, you put it first. When a safe, respectful classroom environment is created, it frees up students to learn at a faster rate. Additionally, those all-important, mandated, standardized test scores *will* automatically improve when students feel good about themselves and with each other.

- How do I even begin to teach this?

> One word at a time . . .
> One egregious act at a time . . .
> One student at a time . . .

Remember, "We are only as great as how we treat the least amongst us." Always encourage understanding, caring, and kindness for those with lesser abilities. Actively teach students how to develop inner-strength skills to deal with teasing, taunting, and discrimination. Read to students the stories of real people who overcame obstacles to become successful. When appropriate, educators can share stories of their own youth and challenges. Search for stories of young people who made a difference in their schools, their communities, and the world.

Anyone Can Make a Difference

Wilma Rudolph, the famous Olympic runner once said, "My doctor told me I would never run. My mother told me I would. I chose to believe my mother."

Dr. Ben Carson, famous chief of neurosurgery at Johns Hopkins University Medical Center, also had a mother who believed in him. Sadly, he was labeled as learning disabled and faced severe racial discrimination from his *teacher!* He, too, chose to believe his mother. He became the lead surgeon on the first team to successfully separate twins co-joined at the head. His life story, *Gifted Hands*, is highly recommended.[9]

Coach Carter believed in his entire team and demanded that they all achieve good grades before playing basketball. The movie based on his true story tells of how he took on the administration and the entire community when he locked the gym until all of his athletes raised their grades and class attendance up to the levels indicated in the "contracts" they had signed with him.[10]

A fifth grader named Taylor questioned his mother about a homeless man on a cold night. As a result, he started a countywide blanket drive that has continued to this day (ten years, at the time of this writing). His sister, Demitria, regularly helps the local women's shelter by gathering back-to-school supplies for the many children who live at the shelter.

Young or old, famous or relatively unknown, there are countless stories such as these where a parent or teacher inspired youngsters to far greater success and inner strength than anyone would have thought possible.

As we grow as unique persons,
we learn to respect the uniqueness of others.
—Robert H. Schuller

Promoting High Self-esteem

Children with high self-esteem are much less likely to pick on other students than those who think little of themselves. True self-esteem is not acquired by giving every child a "gold star." It is found, however, in recognizing the "golden worth" inherent in every child, and reinforcing that for them. One way to help students with this is to help them set long-term goals. Those children who have no such goals are much more likely to drop out of school than those who are clear and passionate about their life plans. Helping to light a fire for their dreams is a way to ensure their success. (For a simple goal-setting project, refer to *Appendix B.*)

Teaching students self-discipline and a sense of duty or responsibility toward others contributes to their self-esteem. So does educating them about the importance of delayed gratification vs. immediate gratification. But, perhaps the most important contributor to a student's self-esteem is to offer them challenges in the classroom that push them beyond their comfort zones. It is with struggle, then success, that students find their inner worth. *Every student* deserves to be challenged, and led to success. Not only does it build self-esteem, but it is the job of every educator to do so (For more on this, see chapter 10 on Rigor).

Another aspect of self-esteem is to teach students that ultimately, *no one can make us think less of ourselves.* Everyone always has the choice to accept or reject the thoughts and opinions of others. Teaching this skill to students and reinforcing it daily offers them a powerful tool for coping with life. Those choices ultimately determine one's happiness and success. For more detailed information on this concept, refer to "E + R = O" in the Appendix of any one of the *Chicken Soup for the Soul in the Classroom* books by Canfield, Hansen, and Unkovich.[11]

Students need to know that *every* negative thought they hold will physically weaken them. In order to experience success, one must hold positive, successful thoughts in his or her mind. When negative thinking occurs, one must immediately cease those thoughts (a visual image of a stop sign, or a halting hand helps this process). Then, the old thought must be replaced with a new, positive thought and image. Our mind *sees* things in pictures, so these images become very important for new behaviors to manifest. A wonderful example of the power of negative thinking is the kinesiology demonstration found in the Appendix of *Chicken Soup for the Soul in the Classroom*, by Canfield, Hansen, and Unkovich.[12]

Every person has the power to stop a bully from physically or emotionally harming another classmate. All it takes is saying:

> "Stop that!"
> "We don't do that here."
> "That is inappropriate."
> "Leave him/her alone!"

The more people who oppose the bully's actions at every juncture, the sooner the behavior will stop. It all goes back to creating a sense of a classroom *family,* where each person watches out for everyone in the group.

It is important to recognize that even *adults* experience peer pressure, and it is often the power of numbers that determines the choices that they make. When teachers share some of these appropriate situations, it helps to increase bonding with their students. It also allows the students to see their instructors as human beings who understand some of the pressures that young people are facing.

It is also essential to go beyond simply showing *respect* for others. Being part of a society also demands having a certain *responsibility* to fellow classmates and peers (see chapters 7 and 8 on Responsibility).

Respect for Possessions

When students have self-respect and a healthy respect for others, respect for possessions will automatically follow.

The process starts with keeping their desk or locker graffiti-free and garbage-free. It spreads to classrooms, hallways, the cafeteria, and the entire school. Eventually, respect for what we have been given encompasses communities, countries, and Mother Earth. This level of respect is the desire to uphold the highest of standards, to maintain a quality of life, and to take a measure of pride in all that one is and all that one does. It is the utmost of respect—the respect for self *and* all that is beyond us.

The Goal of this Chapter

The authors' intention here was to encourage you make respect an integral part of every classroom by presenting some prompts to help you incorporate the teaching of respect in the words you speak and in every action that you expect from your students—to make it something that is ever-present and passed on from person to person, beyond the classroom.

Isn't that the ultimate goal of education—to teach children in a way that *they* will change the world for the better?

If we are persistent as educators, it *will happen* . . .

> one kind word at a time . . .
> one respectful act at a time . . .
> one student at a time . . .

Chapter 5 Thought Starters

1. List ways that *you* exhibit self-respect. Following each item on your list put a **Y** if it is something that may be witnessed and adopted by your students. Put a **N** if it is not, perhaps because it is private, or perhaps because it is simply inappropriate.

Ways you show **self-respect** — Yes or No, if it can be witnessed by students

_____

_____

_____

_____

_____

_____

_____

Remember that for many of these youngsters, **you** are *the only role model* that they have for positive behavior. You are the *hero* for them that stands to pass the test of time. . . .

2. Think back through your life to all of those parents, teachers, family members, and friends who told you something negative about yourself that you *chose* to believe. Now, imagine some all-powerful entity who tells you the opposite. Could you now *choose* this *new* belief? List some of these thoughts below, particularly those that have affected who you are as an educator:

    Old Message: *"You are stupid and can never doing anything right!"*

_____

_____

_____

_____

_____

_____

_____

    New Belief: *"You are very capable and highly successful!"*

_____

_____

_____

_____

_____

_____

_____

For more information about a simple, but powerful tool for releasing old fears and beliefs, read Hale Dowskin's *Sedona Method*.[13]

Chapter 6

Some Fundamentals of the Respectful Classroom

Never doubt that a small group of thoughtful, concerned citizens can change the world; indeed, it's the only thing that ever does.
—Margaret Mead

The Fundamentals of Respect

Quality student-teacher relationships are closely related to how teachers organize their classroom and how they teach their content. A positive classroom atmosphere is critical to academic success.

Fundamental #1—Respectful classroom settings allow students to take an active part in their education. Rules without relationships will breed rebellion.

The following example will demonstrate this point:

A young teacher named, Mr. Smith, was sitting at his desk looking around his empty classroom before the first day of the start of a new school year. He was hoping that this year would be much better than his first year.

Mr. Smith had trouble with classroom control and getting the students motivated to learn and do their work. Homework was like pulling teeth and there were daily classroom disruptions. He was exhausted and discouraged at the end of every school day.

Vowing that this year was going to be different, he decided to "lay down the law" on the first day of school, feeling certain that would ensure a classroom much more conducive to learning

On the first day of class, Mr. Smith stood at the door and ushered his students into class. All students had their names on a desk and they were told to find their seats, sit down, and be quiet. When the bell rang to start class, he introduced himself and immediately stated, "I have decided upon rules that will make this class a better learning environment for all." He went on to say, "If you obey these rules there will be no problems. If you choose not to obey these rules you *will* have a problem!" He then proceeded to hand out a copy of the rules to each student. He called on one student at a time to read the rules aloud as he stressed the consequences for violating each rule. The rules were as follows for *all students*:

1. You will be in your seat and quietly doing work before the bell rings for the start of class. If not, you will be marked tardy. You will receive a detention on your second tardy.
2. You are not allowed to leave your seat without permission. After two warnings in one week, you will receive a detention.
3. You will speak only when called on by the teacher. Speaking out of turn, blurting out answers without being called on, or interrupting in any manner will not be tolerated. After one warning, a detention will be assigned.
4. Failure to turn in homework will not be tolerated. If homework is not turned in on time, you will receive a lunch detention and will be required to finish the assignment during that time. If you don't finish, a grade of "F" will be given for the assignment, and I will contact your parents.

As the first week of classes ended, things were much easier for him, and Mr. Smith was not experiencing the problems he had faced during his first year of teaching. However, as the first month of school passed by, he acquired an uneasy feeling. Although his classroom was *in control,* he sensed that something very important was missing.

Mr. Smith carpooled to school every day with a veteran colleague named, Ms. Jones. She noticed that Mr. Smith was losing the passion he had for teaching when he first arrived at the school, and decided to ask him how his school year was going. "It is better than last year, I think," replied Mr. Smith. "But, I sense that something really important is missing. I guess I don't see the joy of learning in my students as I had envisioned. My class seems to be drudgery to them. They mostly follow the rules, but they seem to be bored and just going through the motions. Something is missing and I just can't put my finger on it."

Here are some possible reasons why Mr. Smith failed to foster the joy of learning in his classroom:

- Mr. Smith's class was more obedience-oriented than responsibility-oriented.
- Mr. Smith did not recognize that *control* is not the same as *quality education*.

There may have been other things wrong in Mr. Smith's classroom, but he started the new school year by *dictating* expected obedience to his students. They had no input about what they thought was important to make their class a high quality and satisfying learning experience. In other words, education was *being done to them* instead of the students having an active part in the process.

Rules without relationships will breed rebellion. Mr. Smith failed to share *ownership* of the learning experience. All he needed to do was to give students some input into a procedure for collecting papers, one of the classroom rules, or some basic ritual or function in the classroom. For example, Mr. Smith may have presented four classroom rules and given students choices for a fifth rule. The class could then have voted on the rule that would become number five. Most important, it would have been a rule *owned by the students*.

Rules adopted by the students are the rules that seldom are violated. Respectful classroom settings that enhance teacher-student relationships will give the students an active part in their education.

While Mr. Smith was learning how to provide student ownership regarding the classroom *rules*, Ms Jones was offering her students some input on the class *content*.

On the first day of class, she presented them with an outline of the topics for the entire semester. She then indicated, "These are the topics that the District requires me to teach you. However, I am not mandated on the *amount* of time that I spend on each of these issues. Please anonymously pick your top five favorites—the ones where you wish to spend the most time. Put an asterisk next to the one that is the most important to you. Finally, draw a line through any *one* topic that you would rather not study at all. We still need to cover it, but we can simply spend less time on it. I will tally the results from the entire class and give you a tentative schedule of the semester tomorrow." In this way, Ms. Jones gave her students some measure of control over the course, itself, while still honoring the requirements of the District.

If educators talk to young people, they will find that it is rarely the teacher who was *feared* the most, or the one who was the most *brilliant* in his/her chosen academic field, who remains in their minds and hearts, inspiring their learning and growth. Teachers need not be a "buddy" to their students. In fact, it is critical that there be reasonable and appropriate boundaries governing the teacher-student relationship. The previous scenario merely suggests that learning is more likely to occur in a *caring and humane environment*.

Real Stories: Most Desired Teacher Qualities

At one Michigan high school, seniors are given an exit interview during their last week of school to get feedback regarding the quality of education they felt they received. One of the items asked was about "most desired teacher qualities." Students were given several choices to rate in order of importance. The following items ranked in the top five every year:

1. A sense of humor
2. Kindness
3. Fairness
4. Willing to help
5. Explains assignments

"Has a strong subject area knowledge," never made the top five. This does not undermine the importance of teacher expertise.

> However, the lesson learned is *what a teacher has in his/her heart is more important to students than what is in his/her head.* Stated otherwise, *if you don't have quality relationships with students, it doesn't matter what you know.*

Most schools are structured and function in such a way that the lower grades tend to be more *relationship*-based and the upper grades, particularly high school, take pride in their *content* focus. It is also interesting to note that student feelings of dissatisfaction and alienation seem to start around the fourth or fifth grade and continue to escalate the longer the student stays in school. Could this trend be related to current student dropout rates?

Can teachers be successful *content* educators while still having caring and meaningful relationships with students? Consider the following educational practices that are invaluable in helping students to grow and succeed:

- positive relationships with students
- understanding and working with a variety of learning styles
- knowing and addressing some of the fears, anger, and anxieties that students bring to the classroom
- being aware of the social patterns that impact students

> *A student never forgets an encouraging private word, when it is given with sincere respect and admiration.*
> —William Lyon Phelps

Fundamental #2—Respectful classrooms have a strength-based focus as opposed to a problem-based focus.

Understanding that the way a teacher views his or her students can make a qualitative difference in student behavior and success is important to the discussion of defining quality relationships. Aside from understanding some of the basic issues that drive many young people, a more effective way of helping them to thrive is by shifting from a problem-focused approach to a strength-based or asset-based approach.

The Strength-based Approach

This approach was developed by Dr. H. Stephen Glenn over the last 20 years of working with students in a positive and strength-based manner.[1] He initially developed the ideas by observing families in a variety of settings where children were thriving in environments that seemed unlikely to produce capable young people. For example, he studied a single-parent mother who was living with her six children in the midst of an extremely high-risk neighborhood in a borough of New York City. This environment is filled with crime, drugs, prostitution, low income and substandard housing. Yet Dr. Glenn found families, like this one, where children avoided these difficulties. In fact, they finished high school, went on to college training, and ended up with good careers and meaningful, productive lives. He found many similar examples in urban, suburban, and rural settings. Obviously, they possessed some strength and skills that helped them to develop into capable young people.

Through his work with these families, Dr. Glenn identified perceptions and skills that children need in order to respond effectively to difficult or challenging situations, and are essential elements of character, resiliency, behavioral health, maturity, and self-sufficiency. They include:

- a strong sense of self-competence and self-control.
- knowledge that they are valued by significant people in their lives.
- strong interpersonal and communication skills to help make friends and interact well with others.
- good judgment to evaluate situations and respond appropriately and with integrity.

There may have been many others who posited such concepts even earlier than Dr. Glenn, but he is the first to clearly and succinctly identify and utilize *strength-based* characteristics with young people. Furthermore, he inspired many educators and human service workers to alter the way they perceived and worked with young people.

Fundamental #3—Respectful classrooms are where teachers re-think or re-frame the way they interact with students.

Someone once said, "The student's perception of the teacher's perception as to whether the student can be successful is more powerful than the student's own perception of whether or not he/she can be successful." In other words, if the teacher *thinks* the student will not be successful, the student will pick up on this perception and probably will not succeed. One of the most powerful qualities that the teacher has is his/her *attitude*. Teachers must believe that all students can learn. Teachers must also believe that every student has a *right* to be in their classroom and that their job is to teach *all* students and put them *all* in a position where they can experience success. *Fairness is not treating all students the same. Fairness is putting everyone in a position for success.* (For more on the positive expectations of teachers, return to Chapter 3, Real Stories: Self-Fulfilling Prophecy or go to Chapter 10, Real Stories: A Match Made in Heaven.)

Evaluations of the Teacher

Another aspect of re-thinking classroom interaction is the regular use of evaluations. The educational system has become so focused on evaluating students with the multiple assessment tests required in many states, and now the NCLB (No Child Left Behind Act)mandated by the federal government, that educators rarely question *themselves*. Nor, do teachers give students the opportunity to assess their instructors in a manner that facilitates *teacher* improvement.

The following assessments and guidelines are recommended:

1. At the beginning of the school year or semester, set goals and rules *with input from the students.*
2. Three or four weeks into the class, provide students with a simple assessment of the course content, as well as the instructional

85

style and fluency of the teacher. This is far enough into the class for teachers to have bonded with most of their students, and should only take 5-10 minutes of class time to complete.

3. At the end of every semester, students should be afforded the opportunity to evaluate both the teacher and the class. Using this information when planning any future classes improves the overall quality of education.
4. Always make these evaluations anonymous.
5. Please put your ego aside as you look for any repeated patterns in ratings or comments. The important thing is to be *open* to suggestions for improvement.
6. Remember that students are regularly assessed. When you give them the same input and opportunity, it contributes to the bonding process.

Fundamental #4—Quality classrooms foster respect for ALL students

Teach the Students You Have

In a respectful classroom, teachers must educate the students they have, not the ones they wish they had. Every classroom has a diversity of students and the playing field is not level. Students will vary greatly in:

- their academic achievement
- their personal grooming
- their interest in the subject being taught
- their personal and social life
- their attitude about school
- their beliefs and commitment regarding their own success
- their coping skills
- their organizational skills
- their personality

The teacher who fosters respect in the classroom must have this attitude; *"It is not about the challenges that the students bring to my class. Rather, it is about what I am going to do about the challenges."* In essence, **it is the teacher's attitude and personal commitment to help every student that**

will determine a respectful classroom. The teacher who builds quality relationships with students will have a caring, respectful classroom.

Working with Students who are Different

A high-needs student (one with ADHD, attachment issues, or other personal problems) is simply different. Not bad, not intentionally demanding, just different. When a teacher can keep this distinction in mind, working with a high-needs child is much easier. (Return to Chapter 4, or go to *Appendix A* for a more detailed discussion and an activity regarding "wounded" students.)

> *Every human being, of whatever origin, of whatever station,*
> *deserves respect.*
> *We must each respect others even as we respect ourselves.*
> —Ulysses S. Grant

Fundamental #5—Respectful classrooms involve assisting youth in behavioral change by positive use of consequences as opposed to punishment.

Respect is more important than obedience. With respect, obedience will happen for the right reasons. Understanding and collaboration are the vehicles that are much more likely to facilitate growth, learning, and change than directive, commanding, or force-orientated approaches. Catch students doing something "right," and reinforce this with some kind of acknowledgment. Noticing something positive, without commenting, is like wrapping a present without giving it. All of this requires setting appropriate boundaries and the establishment of appropriate and healthy limits on behaviors.

A final comment on this issue of consequences and rules: It is extremely important for teachers to *pick their battles*. One teacher in a room full of students cannot possibly deal with everything.

Real Stories: Happy-Grams

Before the days of computers and clip-art, Anna made up a series of five or six drawings and messages that she printed out on bright yellow paper. One had a big smiley face with the comment, "I'm happy to tell you . . ." Another had a funny little frog that said, "Jumping for joy to tell you . . ."

Her goal was to mail one of these simple communications *every day*. With approximately 125 students each day, and semester-long classes, Anna was able to send them to approximately half of her students by the end of their time together.

These notes didn't usually go to the "brightest and best." More often, she sent them to the student who was regularly in trouble, but had a good day, to one who contributed something particularly positive, or to the quiet kid who was never noticed. Occasionally, one went to one of those "brightest" students who did something especially *nice, thoughtful, or caring* for a classmate that day.

Initially, Anna did this so that she could end each day with something positive for *herself*. As a brand new teacher, she was often overwhelmed and filled with doubt. This was a simple way to feel good about her teacher-self.

It didn't take long before Anna realized the payback in the form of a deeper connection with her students. Even the seniors enjoyed getting these notes that were often just a single sentence. The District paid for the postage, and was happy to do so, for their "payback" came in the form of greatly increased positive parent feedback.

Punishment

Every behavior has a *consequence*, either good or bad. You are encouraged to banish the word "punishment" from classroom management, and to replace that concept with one of "behavior—>consequence."

There are many reasons why punishment, in and of itself, is not a viable methodology, particularly in the long term.

- Punishment undermines the whole idea of collaborative asset development.
- Punishment undercuts trust because of the resentment it arouses.
- Punishment moves ownership *from the student to the teacher*.
- Punishment diminishes student motivation to learn.
- Punishment fails to foster responsibility and cooperation.
- Punishment expresses power of *authority*.
- Punishment can be arbitrary or seemingly unrelated to the "crime."
- Punishment implies moral judgment.

Educators get little positive return from the punitive approaches that schools have been using for centuries. In-school suspension time removes a student from the classroom, resulting in the student getting further behind in understanding what was taught in his/her absence. The student is ultimately returning to the classroom with more problems than when he/she left. At times, a student does have to be removed in order to protect the rights of the rest of the class to get a quality education. However, *removing the student from the classroom should be the last option*.

Negative consequences sometimes change behavior, but they do not change attitude, and it is impossible to punish "attitude." To change one's attitude one must appeal intrinsically to the person.

Building quality relationships feeds the intrinsic *urge* for the individual to change one's attitude in a positive manner. When attitudes change, behavioral change will follow. The punitive approach demeans both the adult and the student, creating more problems for both of them.

Discipline

The purpose of discipline is to *correct behavior*, not to get even with the student. Discipline is supposed to be a learning experience, and should be

89

connected to the misbehavior. Effective discipline allows the *consequences* to teach the lesson. In addition, discipline:

- acknowledges rights and respect.
- is related to the behavior, and makes students accountable for their own behavior.
- implies no moral judgment.
- focuses on present behavior.
- permits choice and the opportunity for students to make their own decisions about what course of action is appropriate.
- clearly separates the *student* from the *behavior.*
- permits students to learn from the natural or social order of events in their school or their community.

Benefits of Discipline Rather than Punishment

Working with *consequences* resulting from discipline, rather than punishment, implies collaboration, trust, openness, give-and-take, and a host of other beneficial interactions. These interactions can be of paramount importance in establishing a respectful school environment.

Fundamental #6—Respectful classrooms are caring and personable environments.

In a respectful classroom, the teacher cares about the students, and the students care about the teacher and about each other. There is a comfortable and safe feeling, much like a good home and family. There is a sense of warmth whenever you enter the room. There will be laughter and an experience of joyfulness in learning. Kindness and fairness are always evident. There is a willingness to help on the part of the teacher and a desire to please on the part of the student. There is also an open and honest communication between all participants. There is a desire to succeed on the part of the students and encouragement to succeed coming from the teacher. Both students and teacher simply *like* to be there.

Those who are lifting upward and onward
are those who encourage more than criticize.
—Elizabeth Harrison

Chapter 6 Thought Starters

1. Begin compiling questions that you would ask on a class evaluation. Perhaps you want a simple rating system. Perhaps, you have some follow-up questions that require short answers. Sometimes, a series of smiley, or frowning faces works best, especially for younger students. Encourage students of every age to avoid criticism that lacks solution. If they have a complaint, how would they like to see it fixed? Also, it is important to discuss with your students the fact that some things that we dislike in life are simply unavoidable (e.g. those hated story problems!). Learning *tolerance* may be the important lesson.

   Begin your four-week or final evaluation below, and continue adding to it until it feels like a good assessment. You are further encouraged to discuss possible questions with colleagues.

   _____
   _____
   _____
   _____
   _____
   _____
   _____
   _____

2. Think about yourself as an educator. Will you adapt, change, or work harder for someone who berates you, is sarcastic, or constantly criticizes your teaching style or innovative classroom ideas? Or, are you more willing to change or work harder for an administrator who cares, supports and believes in you?

3. What are the non-negotiable issues in your classroom? Are you ready to *consistently* reinforce them?

Part Four

Responsibility

Chapter 7

Defining Responsibility—Whose Job Is It?

Man blames most accidents on fate—but feels more
personal responsibility when he makes a
hole-in-one on the golf course.
—Unknown

Classroom Responsibility in the 1800s

Nineteenth-century teachers were expected to teach subject matter. Students were expected to do their lessons and to learn. Parents were expected to socialize their children, and to enforce punishment whenever the children didn't do their part. Moral, ethical, and civic responsibility were all taught in the home, and keeping commitments to others was expected. Roles, and the responsibilities within those roles, were clearly defined within the family, the school, and society.

Classroom Responsibility Today

One can hardly discuss *respect* for others without including *responsibility*—a moral, legal, or mental accountability, or as Thomas Lickona refers to it in his book, *Education for Character*,[1] it is our "ability to respond" to others. Respect and responsibility are partners in education—the *yin* to the *yang*, the *right* to the *left*, the *up* to the *down*, the *tit* to the *tat*.

Essentially, when individuals have respect for others, they care about their welfare, and exhibit this in the following ways:

95

- honesty—being genuine, sincere, and truthful; what one says is what one means, and other people can trust that
- perseverance—not quitting people or tasks; continuing until the job is done, despite difficulties or setbacks
- acceptance—treating others with dignity, despite differences in beliefs; exhibiting courtesy and kindness; tolerance; listening
- dependability—being reliable; others can count on you to work to the best of your ability

Deriving from this respect is our feeling of responsibility toward others—to have a sense of obligation to them—family, school, community, and the world. Additionally, the definition of responsibility includes being *accountable* for our behavior, or for tasks accomplished.

> *None of us is responsible for all the things that happen to us,*
> *but we are responsible for the way we act when they do happen.*
> —Unknown

100% Responsibility

If one were to interview highly successful people, many of them will report that you must take 100% responsibility for yourself and for everything you have experienced in your life. You must give up all of your excuses, stop the "blame game," and realize that *you*, and *only you*, will hold the responsibility for your success, happiness, and even health.

Dr. Robert Resnick is credited with the following formula:

$$E + R = O$$

(Event + Response = Outcome) [2]

Simply put, it is only by changing your *responses* to *events* that you can change *outcomes*. When you do, you are taking 100% responsibility for the results you are experiencing in your life. Changing the *thoughts* of today affects the *actions* of tomorrow.

Place this concept into a school system. Who is responsible for success in the classroom? If every person, from the office staff, to the custodial staff, to the administration, to teachers and students, took 100% responsibility for the emotional climate of the school, the care of the buildings, and the success of its students, what would school be like?

> *Let every man shovel out his own snow and the whole city*
> *will be passable.*
> —Ralph Waldo Emerson

Working at 100%

No one can *really* work at 100%, can they? Perhaps it is unrealistic to think of operating at 100% performance for 100% of the time. Certainly, everyone needs some "down time." However, that "down time" needs to be clearly separated from "time on task," and *time on task* needs to have one's full attention and greatest effort.

When you think of the concept of "time on task," think about this: Don't you want *others* to be at 100% when dealing with you?

- your dentist who is doing a complicated root canal in your mouth?
- your pediatrician who is assessing the 104° temperature of your new baby?
- the semi-truck driver in the lane behind you during heavy, speeding traffic?
- the pilot of your plane on your vacation trip to Hawaii?
- the chef at your favorite restaurant . . . or, your *least* favorite restaurant?
- the teenage driver rapidly approaching the stop sign to your left, with a hot pizza to deliver?
- the construction worker who is building your dream home?
- the mechanic who is fixing the brakes on your car?
- the editor of your first book?

Everyone has heard of the horror stories of the train wreck where several people died because the engineer had been on drugs; or, the twenty-car pile-up because a driver was on a cell phone; or, the ferryboat that crashed into the dock, killing people, because the captain of the boat was sleep-deprived; or, the hundreds of deaths each year because of drinking drivers.

None of those people who were responsible for those accidents was 100% on task. Far from it. It is important here to note the two sides to this coin, this definition—that of being responsible *for*, or the cause of something such as a car accident, or a crime. And, that of being responsible *to* others, or being able to answer for one's conduct, choosing between right and wrong, or being reliable and trustworthy in our interactions with others. The first definition tends to be negative, and the second one, more positive.

For the purposes of teaching *responsibility,* the focus here will be on setting examples of *reliability, trustworthiness, and accountability* in all things said and done, and actively teaching these values when possible.

Let's return to this issue of being accountable for one's actions, specifically of being on task, and the "duty" to work at one's best. How would you feel about others being 98% on task? Is that good enough—

- for a brain surgeon?
- for an airline pilot?
- for the air-traffic controller in the tower?
- for a general on the battlefield?
- for the private guarding the compound?
- for a mother who is on her cell phone while driving a van filled with 8-year-old soccer players?
- for an ambulance driver racing through the intersection in front of you?
- for your child's kindergarten teacher?

Ninety-eight percent sounds pretty reasonable, until it directly affects you. What if it is *your child* who falls into the 2% *not* receiving proper attention and education from the kindergarten teacher?

The only thing necessary for the triumph of evil
is for good men to do nothing.
—Edmund Burke

A Crisis of Conscience

In 2009, the entire world found itself in an economic crisis unlike anything since the Great Depression. Far more serious, however, is the "crisis of conscience"—a coined phrase indicating the lack of conscience or feeling of responsibility toward others. Although the originator of this phrase is unknown, some recent examples of the principle are easily citable:

- AIG executives throwing a party on bail-out money
- the misuse of billions of dollars of charity monies for personal gain
- the building and testing of nuclear weapons despite bans and potential world destruction
- the chemical pollution of water, soils, and air by industries trying to make a buck
- multi-million-dollar executives taking huge bonuses while their shareholders lose entire retirement savings accounts
- politicians who give themselves raises or medical benefits while denying them to their constituents
- smokers who pollute the air and drop their cigarette butts for others to clean up
- the use of child labor to produce cheaper products
- individuals who ignore leaky faucets, collectively causing thousands of gallons of water to be wasted
- irresponsible use of limited earthly resources, or contributing to global warming
- witnessing illegal or violent acts and doing nothing to report them or to stop them
- turning our eyes away from genocide or ethnic cleansing, or extreme poverty in *other* parts of the world.

What does any of this have to do with responsibility in the classroom? Consider that it might have *everything* to do with it. Just as this book has repeatedly encouraged you to create a "classroom family," the authors also believe that we are all part of a "global family"—a single humanity. Our birth family teaches us our most profound lessons, both positive and negative. As children begin attending school, it is the "classroom family" that teaches our connectedness to the world—our *responsibility* to others.

> *No snowflake in an avalanche ever feels responsible.*
> —Francois-Marie Arouet

Part of the Solution? . . . Or, Part of the Problem?

Educators who do nothing to create positive change in the world, who stay in their comfort zones and simply allow the *status quo* to continue, are in essence a part of the problem. Teachers change the world, one student at a time. It can be for better . . . or for worse. Like the snowflake in the avalanche in the previous quote, educators need to be mindful of the role they play in students' lives. To not be a part of the solutions *is* to be a part of the problem.

Real Stories: The Violence Movie

Anna showed a classroom video illustrating the power of the media to create certain behaviors in people. It covered things such as the role of advertising in our selection of clothing, the amount of violence in cartoon shows, the placement of advertising to target the young, the *excitement* of violence created for movies, and even the amount of violence regularly witnessed on an evening newscast.

A part of the video showed some historic news clips of actual violence such as that of the Rodney King rioting in Los Angeles. Anna was shocked at the response of guffaws, machismo, and laughter coming from the eighth grade boys witnessing these real and violent beatings.

She stopped the video to share her horror and dismay at *their* reaction and behavior relating to someone being beaten to death—this

---

was *not* a cop show, nor a thriller movie, but a *real person* being shown on the screen.

When she resumed the video, despite her admonishment, the boys could barely contain themselves, and the girls were now giggling, as well. She again stopped the video, choosing this time to *listen* to her students, rather than to sermonize.

"What do you find so *funny* about this?" she asked.

In essence, they found violence to be exciting and fun. That may be explained, in part, by testosterone. But, what about the twittering girls? It turned out that *their* motive was mostly laughing at the boys who were getting in trouble.

In their own way, each group was using these acts of violence to *impress* each other. Furthermore, it was no more "real" to them than any movie or TV show they may have watched. They were so desensitized to the violence that they lacked any empathy for the real people involved.

They continued to discuss how the real person in that video could easily have been their father, brother, or best friend . . . or, it could have been *them!* Violence happens to *real people*, just like themselves. With enough discussion, they finally *got it!*

Anna then turned to the giggling girls, pointing out how *their behavior* merely encouraged the boys to continue with inappropriate and sometimes harmful behavior.

They further discussed how each of them has the ability and the responsibility to put an end to violence . . . one act at a time . . . and one person at a time. And, *"if you aren't part of the **solution**, perhaps you are a part of the **problem**."* That became a motto for the remainder of Anna's teaching years.

We increase our ability, stability, and responsibility
when we increase our sense of
accountability to others on this planet.
—Unknown

Everything that individuals do has some kind of impact on others and/or the environment, either positive or negative.

- Begin by noticing what *you* are doing, and whether it is a part of a *solution*, or a *problem*.
- Be ever mindful of being a role model for your students, both in and out of the classroom.
- Actively teach students to become better citizens by introducing them to ways that they can change the world. (For more, see chapter 8, Teaching Responsibility).

The School-Family Partnership

One can expect, or hope for, these basic values to be taught in the home:

Honesty	Cooperation	Justice
Responsibility	Tolerance	Punctuality
Commitment	Character	Sincerity
Fairness	Ambition	Gratitude
Hard work	Commonsense	Integrity
Charity	Courtesy	Kindness
Dependability	Forgiveness	Equality
Self-discipline	Generosity	Faith
Respect	Humility	Hope
	Perseverance	

The family is clearly the main choice to instill values. But, it is the responsibility of the school to reinforce these values—not necessarily in a sermon-style format, but in the modeling of daily tasks, with an occasional behavior-lecture when a classroom situation deems it necessary. The book, *Educating for Character: How Our Schools Can Teach Respect and Responsibility* by Thomas Lickona provides numerous stories, examples, and opportunities to teach values and character at every level, and urges schools to make this a priority. Lickona's book also cites many statistics regarding failing societal values, and the absolute *need* to *teach* values in our educational institutions.[3]

Schools should consider it to be their primary "responsibility," and should take a leadership role to actively teach the value of *responsibility*. Because the school is the primary site for almost all social interactions, it is the perfect place to educate youth about Lickona's definition of responsibility—this *ability to respond to others*. School is also the first "job" that a student will have, again presenting an opportunity to teach the importance of responsibility.

Whether it is in the home, school, community, or world, the responsible person:

- takes charge and does what needs to be done
- is 100% accountable for his or her actions
- can be counted on to fulfill obligations
- offers results, not excuses
- makes choices based on what is *right*, not what is *easy*

Ideally, a solid partnership between family and school will be the factor that successfully socializes children in their feelings of responsibility.

> *Responsible persons are mature people*
> *who have taken charge of themselves and their conduct,*
> *who own their actions and own up to them—*
> *who answer for them.*
> —William J. Bennett

Responsibility is an Attitude *and an* Action.

As a society, we count on others to do the right thing. In fact, our very lives depend on:

- driving on the right side of the road
- stopping at stop signs or red lights
- following the speed limits
- not robbing nor raping
- not harming people nor property

Essentially, laws are established to protect our rights as humans, and *responsible* people will follow these societal rules and will make choices because it is the *right* thing to do.

However, we seem to be evolving into a society that takes the *easy* way, rather than the *right* way—that follows rules only when others are looking and there is a possibility of getting "caught." Even worse, many young people today think something is wrong *only* if they do get caught!

We may count on others to be responsible, but there is no reward for doing what is right, merely consequences for doing something wrong. Both parents and educators are in the unique position to "catch" children doing the right things, and to reinforce the value and the importance of this. Ultimately, it is the task of significant adults to instill this "rightness" at such a level that the rewards are *intrinsic*, or come from within—that it simply *feels good* to do what is *right*.

The challenge is even greater because there are so few heroes anymore—people who are seemingly perfect in character to a child growing up.

Note what today's children witness on a daily newscast:

- top athletes using performance-enhancing drugs, and lying about it
- parents being thrown out of arenas for unsportsmanlike behavior at their child's athletic events
- perpetrators pleading "not guilty," hoping to get away with their crime or to receive reduced sentencing
- people suing others just to make an "easy buck"
- politicians having affairs because they have the "power" to do so
- people blaming others rather than accepting responsibility for their own mistakes

Children at very early ages already know right from wrong. At virtually every age, their decision to commit an act depends primarily on whether they might get caught, and ultimately on whether they will get punished, or may lose the affection of their parents.

Obviously, the strongest influence in this teaching is their parents. There is a saying that "the apple doesn't fall too far from the tree," meaning that the child will most likely exhibit the values and behaviors of the parents.

The next level of influence is that of their *respected teachers.* Because teachers have such a powerful impact, it is their job to communicate their expectations regarding the responsibility of *doing* what is right vs. what is wrong. Additionally, educators must hold students accountable by having consequences that mean something. Finally, it is the teacher's *attitude* about right and wrong, and the *strength of their feelings* shown about it that will ultimately instill these values to their students. Once again, it is the *relationship* that teachers have with their students that is the basis for learning.

Hopefully, parents are doing their job by instilling the importance of responsibility. Even if they are not doing so, *teachers* still have the power to make a huge difference in this arena *if* they have built a quality relationship with their students. Never underestimate the power that teachers have to make this impact on their students, and ultimately, on the world. Children learn right from wrong by example, not merely instruction. Educators can teach, *and* show, and practice the *action* component of responsibility. And, they can further encourage the *attitude* element.

Believe in yourself.
Believe in your own potential for greatness.
Believe that you can change the world.
It is something that is within reach of all of us.
—Evan Michael Tanner

In the information presented so far, it has been suggested that real changes are needed to help develop new ways of working with young people. For some, this can be very difficult. It is normal human behavior to adopt explanations or rationalizations that support behaviors with which we feel most comfortable. These rationalizations must be addressed if any meaningful change is to occur.

So in addition to recognizing the unique ways of seeing and functioning in the world, one must also acknowledge that excuses and justifications for behavior are very real and powerful. This suggests that both the teacher and the student must exhibit a good deal of honesty in addressing less than functional behaviors. If this concept can be owned and implemented in a collaborative way, positive changes are more likely to occur. This behavioral change and growth is best accomplished by sharing the journey.

*Change will not come if we wait for some other person
or some other time.
We are the ones we've been waiting for.
We are the change that we seek.*
—President Barack Obama

Responsibility—Whose Job Is It?

It is one thing to model and to teach the *concept* of responsibility, but ultimately, who in society *holds* the *responsibility* for doing something? Who holds the responsibility for change? Who holds the responsibility for quality education, for improved test scores, for happy and successful students? Who holds the responsibility for the protection of the planet, for abolishing hunger, for world peace? Who holds the responsibility for political reform, health reform, financial reform, educational reform?

Who is Responsible for the Education of Our Children?

Parents?	Neighbors?	Politicians?
Custodians?	Siblings?	Religious affiliates?
Teachers?	The President?	Police?
Extended family?	Principals?	Coaches?
Grandparents?	Community leaders?	

This critically important job should not fall on any one or two segments of our society. Rather, *all are responsible*, and everyone should make opportunities to promote, to model, and to teach socially acceptable behaviors for our youth.

While the task of subject-specific content will mostly fall on the shoulders of classroom teachers, the importance of societal values can be taught by anyone. Even *content* can be taught outside of the classroom:

- a cashier in a store can help to teach math by counting back change rather than just dumping it in a child's hands.
- the secretary in the school office can help to teach respect by the use, and the expectation of use of the words "please" and "thank you."
- a grandparent can help teach science by exploring tide pools while on an ocean-side vacation, or exploring flora and fauna on a nature hike.

Every single experience that a child has is a learning experience of some sort, as well as an opportunity for someone nearby to teach. Obviously, some people are responsible for certain tasks, but *everyone* is responsible for *something*. And, *anyone* can teach another to care about, or to be responsible for others, or to develop an emotional attachment to doing the right thing. (See chapter 8 on Teaching Responsibility).

The Role of the Parent in Teaching Responsibility

As with everything, the earliest learning of responsibility is acquired in the home, starting when parents assign age-appropriate chores and attach logical consequences. Holding children responsible for tasks that directly affect them usually works best, such as:

- removing their plate from the table following a meal
- care of their own laundry (dirty clothes in the basket, washing their own clothes)
- making their own lunch for school
- cleaning their own room

It is critical that the parents *not* do the work for their children, even if the results are less than perfect. A parent's job is to assign reasonable tasks, to *expect* them to be accomplished in a reasonable time, and to hold children accountable by having reasonable consequences for failure to complete their chores. Responsibility is not taught by protecting children from mistakes. Rather, it is accomplished by expecting responsible behavior and disciplining fairly and with love when mistakes do occur.

This is a learning experience for children that will help them to manage their time and their tasks, and is a skill they will use throughout life. These early skills translate to the classroom environment when children start attending school. As they learn to manage chores at home, they learn to manage their time, their tasks, and their lives. With this acquired know-how, they will then be more organized, more responsible, and ultimately will be more successful in school.

> *In a free society, all are involved in what some are doing.*
> *Some are guilty, all are responsible.*
> —Abraham Joshua Heschel

What Parents Should Not *Do:*

- remind children of their tasks or chores
- threaten to take away privileges
- bribe children to do their chores or homework
- deliver forgotten lunches
- deliver forgotten books or homework
- complete schoolwork *for* their children, or excessively "help"
- manipulate the system and/or badger the teachers so that the child's "record" looks perfect
- protect children from the consequences of their behavior

Although teachers cannot be responsible for what goes on in their students' homes, they can certainly be observant of these behaviors in parent/child relationships and make efforts to advise against them when appropriate.

Real Stories: The Wrong Lesson Learned

Mitch* was an amazing athlete. He excelled in every sport that he tried, and was certain to get several scholarship offers in the years to come. Because Mitch was so talented athletically, he was often allowed to "slide by" in doing his homework, and achieved below-average grades. That seemed to be okay with everyone. Parents and coaches were happy just to keep him eligible.

At age thirteen, Mitch was drinking a lot. Everyone knew it. No one did anything about it. His parents felt that he was "just being a typical teenager . . . and sowing his wild oats." Again, there were no consequences for his behavior.

However, one night Mitch was at an underage drinking party where the police were called. Because he was a minor, he was released to his parents, and his arrest was legally kept "confidential." When school officials heard of the offense of several of their student-athletes, they called each of them in, with their parents, to deal with this breach of athletic code.

As Mitch was confronted by the principal and athletic director, his parents intervened to say, "Mitch, do not confess to anything! They have no proof, and they cannot remove you from the team without proof."

Mitch did *not* confess. His teammates did, suffered the outcome of a reduced season, and learned the lesson intended—that breaking the rules has consequences.

Mitch continued with his drinking. It became excessive, and drugs became a regular part of his life, as well. He was caught again, and again, and eventually banned from all athletics in the district. As a result, he later ended up in jail, not on a college or pro team, as was his assumed destiny.

Mitch's parents' misguided attempt to *protect* their child from missing out on a few athletic competitions circumvented the lesson of "logical consequences." In the end, it cost Mitch a potentially successful career in sports.

*not his real name.

Every one to whom much is given, of him will much be required.
—Jesus

Real Stories: Sticks and Stones Can Break My Bones *and* Words Can Destroy Me

During his years as an at-risk coordinator, Dave was often asked to speak at conferences, and to give advice to teachers who work with at-risk students. One of the pieces of advice he gave was, "Although it is important to confront students, we need to be careful of what we say and how we say it."

In order to demonstrate the importance of his point, Dave planned to ask ten of the students on his at-risk caseload to share what adults said to them on a regular basis—things that really hurt their feelings and/or caused them to judge themselves as a result. Dave told them that he would be presenting this information at a conference to teachers and other educators who work with people their age. He promised to keep their names confidential, but wanted to use their statements as a caution to adults who may need to confront youth because of inappropriate behavior.

He called each of the students into his office and asked the question, "What do you hear from adults quite often when they confront you about a problem?" With little thought, the students quickly blurted out their responses:
"You're pathetic."
"You can't do anything right."
"I'm sick of looking at your face."
"You disgust me."
"You can't be my kid."

Dave was so depressed after the first five replies that he decided not to ask the next five, as planned. The fifth student who said, *"You can't be my kid,"* broke into tears. Words hit as hard as a fist. Whoever said, "Sticks and stones may break my bones, but words will never hurt me," *lied.*

While it's important to confront students' inappropriate behavior, teachers need to be careful how they do it. If students are hearing these kinds of comments on a regular basis from the people closest to them, it is absolutely critical that they are *not* getting this from their teachers, administrators, or school counselors. Educators must learn to address student *behavior* without destroying the child in the process.

What Parents *Should Do:*

- communicate clearly with their children regarding their expectations for their child's behavior, and consequences for noncompliance
- maintain reasonable communication with teachers so they are operating as a team for the betterment of the child
- arrange for additional help for children having difficulties
- step back and let logical consequences unfold
- be the enforcer of consequences when boundaries have been crossed

Education is a Team Sport

It takes a village to raise a child and a team to educate one. Unfortunately, many parents today do not know how to properly parent their children. Often parents want to be *liked* by their children or to be *friends* with them. This blurs the boundaries and prevents parents from acting in some simple, structured ways as indicated in the previous lists.

Perhaps a graduation requirement for a *parenting* class would provide a stronger leg to this team. In the meantime, it falls on the shoulders of many educators to teach parents how to properly parent their children for success in the school setting. While it is one more thing on the teacher's platter, it is crucial to the teamwork necessary in creating successful students.

Dave Opalewski & Anna Unkovich

Student Responsibilities Regarding School

Young people of every age will step up to expectations when those expectations have been clearly communicated. Assuming that the adults have been doing their part, the student should:

- get themselves up and ready for school
- do their own homework
- study for their own tests
- remember to take books, lunches, and homework to school
- keep track of their own work (school planners, or some kind of planning system)
- be on time for classes and commitments
- be prepared for class (writing utensils, textbooks, homework)
- turn in assignments on time
- treat teachers, school personnel, and classmates respectfully
- ask for help when needed
- communicate bullying or abuse situations
- accept reasonable consequences for failure to meet communicated expectations
- do their best work at all times
- take 100% responsibility for their own successes

The Teacher's Role in Responsibility

Parents set the tone for the family. Superintendents set the tone for the district. Principals set the tone for the school building. And, teachers set the tone for the classroom. How responsible students are, and how successful they will be, will depend on the teacher's expectations for them, how well they communicate those expectations, and whether they consistently follow up with logical and reasonable consequences.

The teacher's job is to:

- *care for students* and students' success
- develop and teach a course content that is challenging and relevant, yet consistent with the district's expectations

112

- clearly communicate course objectives to students
- clearly communicate classroom intentions for student success, including grading criteria and methods, as well as homework, testing, and project expectations
- clearly communicate the attendance policy
- demonstrate and expect respectful behavior between students, and between students and the teacher
- set the tone for a "classroom family"
- involve students in the classroom decision-making process whenever possible including classroom goals and rules
- help students to organize and manage time and tasks for their success
- encourage students to voice thoughts, opinions, and feelings in appropriate ways
- encourage discussions about difficult issues and possible solutions
- maintain meaningful communication with parents (information, expectation, and responsibility for success that is age-suitable)
- execute thoughtful and well-planned lessons that use a variety of teaching methods
- be available and accessible for student questions and help
- clearly set boundaries for parents and students regarding *responsibility* issues
- be consistent in dealing with consequences and discipline issues
- continually communicate student progress, or have a means whereby students have on-going access to their status

Real Stories: Check It Three Times

Anna expected all of her students in grades seven and up to carry and use some sort of planner system—a hand-made planning calendar, or a simple one that was purchased. Eventually, the district purchased school planners for every student, but many students weren't using them or didn't know how to use them properly.

In addition to teaching students *how* to use these organizational tools, she gave them classroom credit if her class assignments were recorded correctly whenever she randomly checked their planners.

She also taught them a "check-three-times" system to use with their planners:

1. ***Check*** before leaving school to make sure you are taking all books and materials home with you.
2. ***Check*** when you first get home to plan the amount of time needed to complete all tasks, and *when* those tasks will be tackled.
3. ***Check*** before leaving for school in the morning to make sure that you have all completed homework with you and ready to turn in.

The division of responsibility presented here is not perfect, but is meant as a guide to encourage students and parents to do their part, so that the teachers can fulfill their segment of the education triangle. When all members do their proper share (each at 100%), it will not add to the "overly-filled teacher's platter." Rather, it should allow more time for educators to focus on the tasks of being a good teacher. It *is* suggested that teachers reprioritize their time and effort, making communication and connection with their students as a top concern.

Chapter 7 Thought Starters

1. List occasions in *your life* where you did/did not do something that became a *problem* for you or for others, particularly in the classroom.

   _____

   _____

   _____

   _____

   _____

   _____

2. Now list times when your actions became a part of a ***solution***.

   _____

   _____

   _____

_____
_____
_____

3. Go back to the list of values found under the heading "The School-Family Partnership." Below, add any values that you were taught, or you would want to be taught in your family:

_____   _____
_____   _____
_____   _____
_____   _____
_____   _____
_____   _____

Is anything on this list different from what you would like to see in your *classroom*?

4. List ways that *you* exhibit responsibility—in your home, your classroom, your community, the world:

_____
_____
_____
_____
_____
_____
_____

Chapter 8

Teaching Responsibility

Tell me and I'll forget.
Show me and I may remember.
Involve me and I'll understand.
—Chinese Proverb

This chapter will discuss some ideas for teaching youngsters to be responsible:

- by responding to and caring for others
- by being accountable for their actions and/or tasks completed

Teaching to Care

Essentially, this is an issue of teaching to the *heart*, not the *head,* and in many ways is mostly an extension of respecting others (refer to chapters 5 and 6 for more comprehensive coverage of this topic). It is not an intellectual concept, but one of empathy, and is designed to reach students of every age by introducing them to the *feelings* of others.

The following* are some ways to tap into students' emotions and to help them to truly connect with others on the planet:

- Imagine being the "other sex." How would your life be different?
- Visit a nursing home. Listen to the stories of those with 70+ years of experience.
- Read stories of people overcoming obstacles. How would you handle those challenges?

- Invite speakers into class who have dealt with personal challenges. What can you learn from their experiences? Can this have an impact on how *you* handle life situations?
- Learn sign language. What would life be like if you couldn't hear? See? Smell? Touch? Taste?
- Go to an ethnic restaurant. Discuss the culture, as well as the food.
- Study a foreign country, its culture and language. What would be the pros and cons of living there?
- Have a school "diversity day," where students and staff dress to represent their heritage. Coordinate with the cafeteria to feature ethnic foods.
- Role play ways to deal with bullies. What are some ways to be safe at school?
- Look for stereotypes in books, magazines, and on television. What do stereotypical messages imply?
- Adopt a classroom charity. Why does it feel good to help others who are in need?
- Promote good sportsmanship. Ban any "trash talking" and uphold severe consequences for such behavior. Start a campaign to educate parents on this issue.
- Watch a movie that taps into the *heart* of another. *Pursuit of Happyness*[1] touches on the issue of homeless children. *Pay It Forward* [2] shows ways to geometrically multiply acts of kindness to touch the world. (As with any media, it is recommended that teachers *preview for suitability.)*
- Regularly use personal and classroom situations to gain understanding of one another.
- Have a poster contest addressing kindness, acceptance, tolerance, or simply diversity.
- Students can end daily announcements with a "positive thought for the day."
- Have a "clean the campus" day where the entire school is involved in the clean-up of trash and graffiti. Or, create a team competition called, "Run for the Garbage" to clean up the athletic fields. Form cleanup teams where the athletes can retrieve and deposit only one item of trash at a time. The team with the highest count receives an easier workout the following day. Cleaning up the trash can be a game as well as a team workout.

*Some of these ideas have been adapted from *101 Tools for Tolerance*.[3] See www.tolerance.org for a wealth of information on celebrating diversity.

> *No exercise is better for the human heart than reaching down to lift up another person.*
> —Tim Russert

Developing Emotional Literacy

The previous list gives a few suggestions for helping students to consistently "walk in each other's shoes." When doing so, teachers are recommended to repeatedly take students to the *heart* of another. Teachers can ask questions that generate the *feeling* component in a situation. They can ask students to consider how the *other person is feeling*. It is most powerful to emotionally put students on the *receiving* end of a situation that they may be prone to create:

- How does it *feel* to be taunted?
- How does it feel to have your bike stolen?
- How does it *feel* to be bullied?
- How does it *feel* to be ignored?
- How does it *feel* to have someone lie to you?
- How does it *feel* when someone talks behind your back?
- How does it *feel* when someone says untruthful things about you or your family?
- How does it *feel* when someone is mean to you?
- How does it *feel* when someone calls you names?
- How does it *feel* when someone puts private information about you on the Internet?

To truly be successful at understanding how another person *feels* in a situation, teachers need to challenge students to dig deeply into these *feelings*. Simply saying, *"it feels bad"* is not enough. Instructors should insist that students be more specific. Find out:

- Does it make you angry?
- Does it make you sad?
- Does it make you hurt?
- Does it make you lonely?
- Does it make you feel rejected?
- Does it make you want to get even?
- Does it make you feel sorry?
- Does it make you feel embarrassed?
- Does it make you feel confused?
- Does it make you feel frustrated?

Where *in your body* do you sense these feelings?

- In your gut?
- In your throat?
- In your chest?
- In your neck and shoulders?
- Do you clench your jaw?
- Do you clench your fists?
- Do you get a headache?
- Do you get a stomachache?

All feelings reside in the human body somewhere. When teachers encourage students to talk about these emotions or to write about them, they are fostering "emotional literacy."

By using this skill of "emotional literacy," students learn to take responsibility for others and care about their welfare despite their differences.

> *When you take responsibility on your shoulders,*
> *there is no room left for chips.*
> —Unknown

Teaching Students to be Accountable

Little by little, we have become an irresponsible society. Adults are regularly called with reminders of medical appointments or scheduled meetings, and have come to *expect* these "memory nudges." Because "time is money," it is difficult to find a doctor anymore who will risk having patients who may miss appointments. Instead, they pay someone on staff to spend countless hours making reminder calls, and then pass this cost onto *all* of their patients. Whatever happened to the concept of making an appointment or scheduling a meeting and then being *committed* to being there?

Having a strong desire to create success for youngsters, parents and educators have inadvertently *created* this monster called "irresponsibility." How many times have parents reminded children to do a certain chore, or have educators reminded students that a specific assignment was due? Did this occur so often that these youngsters no longer felt any responsibility to remember it for themselves?

Did all of this start back in the late 1960s when the concept of "responsibility" was out of favor? Or, when the drugs were so popular that people were "reminded" of things just in case they were "high" and had forgotten? Back in the '50s, there wasn't much evidence of constantly reminding people to do things. There certainly were no reminders to keep simple appointments.

Regardless of when or why it started, the reality is that it has been going on long enough that *adults* now have *expectations* that they will be reminded of things for which they should be responsible.

Breaking Old Habits and Starting New Ones

On a related note, many parents now expect teachers to do much of their parenting for them. Or, they expect teachers to be accountable for their child's success, rather than expecting their child to hold this responsibility.

This leads to two key areas of teaching responsibility:

- that of starting off this next generation with new rules and expectations that will *create* responsible youngsters who will grow up to be responsible adults.

- that of re-educating parents, both in their parent-to-teacher role as well as in their parent-to-child role.

Teachers Are Who They Are, Not What They Do

Before dealing with either of these concepts, the issue of responsibility begins with the *teacher*. Simply *being* a teacher carries a huge responsibility. It is not just showing up and receiving a paycheck. In addition to dealing with self, every teacher is legally and morally responsible for the lives and learning of every one of his or her students. That is a lot to manage.

Teachers can begin by looking at what they say and do and then model responsibility for students every minute of every day.

> *"You can't build a reputation on what you are **going** to do."*
> *Henry Ford*

Real Stories: Dave's Dual Set of Classroom Rules

Dave believed in establishing *few* rules that encompassed *many* appropriate behaviors. He laminated and posted these rules at the front of the classroom:

- Students are required to show respect to **ALL** people.
- Students are to be on time for class.
- Students are required to be prepared for class.
- No food or drink is allowed in the classroom.

Once the rules were posted, Dave had the feeling that something was missing. After some deep inner thought, he created a second bill of rules, laminated it and hung it next to the original list. It read:

- The teacher is required to respect **ALL** people.
- The teacher is required to be on time for class.
- The teacher is required to be prepared for class.
- The teacher is not allowed to eat or drink in the classroom.

When presenting the rules, Dave informed the students that he would hold them responsible for these class regulations, and he asked them to keep him accountable as well.

Re-educating Parents

Following the self-examination that is necessary to be a good and responsible teacher, it is important to get the parents on board with classroom goals for responsible children. This teamwork establishes the foundation on which to build successful education for every child.

With the new generation of parents who *expect* reminders, who *expect* teachers to call with every dip in their child's grade, who *expect teachers* to create their child's success, this could be a difficult task. The key is communication, and thereby holding parents responsible for their part in the education process. Having administrative support is crucial to the success team, as well.

Real Stories: The Letter Home to Parents

As a well-established and well-respected teacher in the community, Anna *acted* on something that was becoming a growing frustration—parents who were taking far too much responsibility for the successes of their children.

The problem was not helped by administrators who were overly anxious to please parents rather than to really look at what was in the best interest of the child. Because it was a "high achieving" community, "grades" and "test scores" were considered to be of the utmost value, *not* necessarily the true learning that was transpiring, nor the love of learning, nor the overall education that the child should be receiving. For many, the goal was the "grade."

This led to high pressures from parents for things to look good on paper, whether or not the child actually did the work. Often the parents excessively "helped" in order to create greater success for the child. Despite the fact that the only grades that remain on a student's record are the final grades, report cards went out every nine weeks, then every six weeks. And then there were "interim reports" at some magical halfway point so that parents would *know* of any problems in advance. Teachers had little time to *teach!* They were constantly filling out grade reports of one kind or another. And, if they had any special education students in their classrooms, the issue of reporting was geometrically multiplied, with daily reports on some students. Those teachers who welcomed special needs children into their rooms were often overwhelmed with the required paperwork.

One year, Anna decided that enough was enough! She devised a plan to put responsibility where it belonged—back on the students. She wrote a letter to parents that indicated the following classroom procedures:

- that the grading scale and explanation of extra credit opportunities were always posted and were included with this letter
- that *all* assignments were listed daily on the chalkboard and on a monthly classroom calendar for students to copy into their planners
- that *verbal* directions would also be given for every assignment and test
- that students were expected to *ask* for make-up work when absent, or for help, when needed
- that every student would be recording all of their assignments and scores into a folder, and that *parents should ask for this folder every weekend*
- that she would *not make phone calls nor send out interim reports indicating failure* (each of those 6-week report cards were the *warnings* to parents)
- that she encouraged the parents to allow their child the *full responsibility* for their grades in the class, but that there should be *family consequences* for poor grades due to assignments not completed
- that she would *welcome* their calls during her available hours to deal with any issues regarding the success or happiness of their child
- that she provided her *home phone* number to students and parents for any *student-related emergencies* (*not* homework)

Parents were expected to sign this letter/contract and they were kept on file in case issues surfaced later on.

A copy of this letter was also given to the principal, along with class rules, syllabus, etc. for the administrators to file.

It didn't take long for parents to appreciate the increased responsibility in their children, and it didn't take long for the students to enjoy the pride and sense of accomplishment of doing their part. Anna rarely had a complaint, and it was easily resolved by showing parents their signature of acknowledgment on this contract.

The Next Generation: New Rules, New Expectations

This section will offer some general concepts on classroom expectations. There are many specific examples of this cited in *Real Stories* throughout the book. The most important thing to remember is when adults do too much for young people, they create a sense of entitlement that robs these youngsters of the experiences in which they can learn responsibility and appreciation for others.

It is recommended that teachers:

- Clearly communicate their expectations on the first day. When things are important, do them first.
- Be prepared for resistance—it is the nature of young people to "test" those in authority.
- "Pick their battles." Decide what is important and non-negotiable. It is better to enforce a few expectations than to have so many that they are overlooked and not enforced.
- Consistently reinforce the concepts stated at the onset. *Allow* the students to experience the natural consequences of their lack of responsibility.
- Introduce students to various ways that they can have an impact on the world: stories or guest speakers to inspire; volunteer work; the *pay it forward* concept; helping others is the anti-depressant that is not a drug; the *feel-good* aspect of assisting others; etc.

- "Practice what they preach." Teachers cannot expect responsibility if they do not model it.
- Create a classroom environment that fosters *living and learning responsibly.*

Creating a Classroom Family

In this book, the authors repeatedly emphasize the importance of creating a classroom *family*—that connection between teacher and students, and between students and their classmates. Students develop a responsibility to the group—the *family*—by *living* it.

With each relationship that is formed, the *classroom family* strengthens. One suggestion is to regularly partner students in different pairs so that they get to know everyone in the classroom. When this is done frequently, students will come to expect it as a part of the classroom routine. If the sessions are kept short, the students are less likely to feel burdened or "stuck" with any given partner for a long period of time. Another suggestion is to use a deck of playing cards to match partners, or some other means whereby no one feels threatened to be the "last one chosen." The important thing is to establish safe ways to create dialogue between classmates.

Another simple way to expose students to each other is to regularly change their seating assignments, perhaps every week. Many books listing these "ice-breaker" types of activities are available—a wise investment of time and money if they help with the task of getting *every* student to know *every other student* in the class.

Highly functional *families* work out problems together. The successful teacher will create a classroom meeting time or system for resolving conflict or dealing with group frustrations or anger. Any time that students can express their *feelings* in a safe way, they will be more connected to those in the group. Circle talks that focus on feelings, and are structured where only one person is allowed to talk at a time, are good ways to create this family dynamic. In addition, problem-solving as a group is a great way to explore options and come up with multiple solutions.

Finally, *families* have similarities that bind them. Teachers can also create situations whereby students can see and experience the things that they have in common, and where they can learn to respect the differences they have. A "people hunt" is a wonderful introductory experience that allows students to examine simple similarities and differences. (See *Appendix A, Part Four* for an example.)

Chapter 8 Thought Starters

1. Evaluate yourself as an example of *responsibility* for your students. Begin by answering the following questions:

   - Are you responsible?
   - Do you consistently model this behavior for students in and out of class?
   - Do you return papers in a timely fashion?
   - Do you promptly begin and end lessons on time?
   - Do you communicate goals and intentions clearly?
   - Do you *expect* students to act responsibly without frequent reminders?
   - Are you consistent in holding students accountable for their work and their behavior?
   - Do you keep promises made to students?
   - Have you done everything possible to create a *classroom family?*

2. Create a student responsibility plan for your classroom. List tasks that you *expect* your students to be responsible for in your class. List consequences for failure to do so. (e.g. homework turned in on time, having books or materials in class, etc.)

Student Responsibility	Consequences for Failure to Comply
_____	_____
_____	_____
_____	_____
_____	_____
_____	_____

_____ _____

_____ _____

Remember that it is more important to have a few things that you will enforce, rather than many that you will ignore.

Part Five

Relevance and Rigor

Chapter 9

Making Education Relevant

*You get the best efforts from others
not by lighting a fire beneath them,
but by building a fire within.*
—Bob Nelson

Educational Relevance in Previous Centuries

In the early years of our country's schools, much of the subject matter studied was not particularly relevant to the students' daily needs. The almost exclusive memorization of verses, history dates, and capital cities (never to be visited), could hardly be considered important life tools to the early settlers. However, instead, they valued knowledge for knowledge's sake. They knew that it was important to *learn*. While reading and simple math might actually be *used*, school overall was considered important for challenging the mind, for learning how to think. The goal was to "graduate" from the eighth grade.

At this time, most males were expected to quit school to work on the family farm. A high school or college degree was considered unnecessary for their survival lifestyle. Females *might* complete high school, but were then expected to marry rather than to pursue further education or employment. The role of the school was *not* to prepare students for the job market, nor for living in their world. Instead, learning was viewed as "nourishment for the soul." It was nice, but not necessary.

Often, families lived several miles from school. Students walked or rode horses in any kind of weather in order to attend. It was a time in history when getting an education certainly wasn't taken for granted. However, education ranked second to survival, and it was common for the boys to miss school when the crops needed to be planted or harvested.

Relevance—What's Important to Students Today?

In today's world of education, decisions are made *for* students regarding what is important to learn. Politicians, long removed from classrooms, set graduation requirements and educators teach to those standards and expected assessments. Rarely are students consulted about what they think is important, or what they might want to learn. Elective classes, the only *choices* that students have, are slowly being eliminated from the school curriculum. This is because there is no time to fit them into schedules and still complete courses that are required for graduation and especially for college entrance. As a result, many students become either bored or frustrated with school as exemplified in the following story:

Real Stories: The Wrong Perception

In his position of "At Risk Coordinator," Dave's major responsibility was working with the student population considered to be at risk for academic failure and/or dropping out of school. Additionally, he worked with the families of these students in an attempt to address the factors creating these difficulties, and brought his 25 years of classroom experience to this strategic job.

As Dave began to work with these academically challenged students, he was astonished to find that more than half of them possessed the basic skills to be academically successful. In fact, when checking their files, he found that more than half of them had scored from average to high on standardized assessments. Additionally, a large number of these secondary students had done fairly well in their early elementary grades.

Through counseling sessions with them, Dave discovered that many had experienced unfortunate life episodes while growing up. Knowing that misfortunes were a factor, he was not convinced that these experiences were a *major* factor in the students' academic struggles. He repeatedly heard similar comments from them:

> *"We never talk about the real world in class."*
> *"Why is this stuff important to know?"*
> *"When will I ever use this?"*
> *"How will this help me get a job?"*

Their problem wasn't a lack of skill, as first perceived by Dave and the other teachers. *These students could not connect what they were taught in the classroom to their world.* In other words, the students failed to see the *relevance* of their formal educational experiences.

The "Blame Game"

One might ask, "Whose fault is it that youngsters see no value in school or are dropping out of school in increasing numbers?" Is it the parents' fault for not making education a priority in the home, or for leaving the responsibility for learning totally up to the classroom teacher? Is it the students' fault for refusing to put forth the effort to learn? Or, is it teachers' fault for not connecting classroom instruction to the real world?

The "blame game" will serve no useful purpose in addressing this situation. Ideally, each element of the educational triangle—the students, the parents, and the school/teacher community—should take 100% responsibility for its part in improving education.

Except for some brief guidelines for parent and student responsibility, this is a book for educators, and optimally, they must take a long hard look at how they teach what they teach. Observing classrooms, one can see how instruction appeals to Baby Boomers or Generation X students. But the present generation of student—the "millennial generation" see their world in a much different light than previous generations. And indeed, *their world is different!*

Who Are The "Corner Kids"?

An April 17, 2009 airing of Bill Moyers featured an interview with David Simons, who talked about the excessive number of people in the United States who are under-educated and not prepared for the world. He referred to these poor, vulnerable, "discarded" citizens as "corner kids," for they are out of the education system and *out* on the street *corners* of America. Indeed, the most viable thing for them to do is to participate in the drug trade on any neighborhood corner in many cities of our country.[1]

According to Simon, in our political, market-based culture, they simply aren't "worth saving." They are the kids that got left behind.

The concern of many educators is that the numbers of "corner kids" are growing, and that the politicians who are making decisions regarding their welfare are so far removed from any classroom that they have no idea how to fix the problem.

When one is sick, he or she seeks a physician. If the car is broken, one goes to a mechanic. Why then, are *politicians* expected to fix *education?* Shouldn't the teachers in the trenches be the first line of defense—the ones with the answers? Shouldn't someone ask the *students* why they are leaving school in droves and causing dropout rates to be in excess of 50% in some communities? Additionally, someone needs to *do something* with the answers received.

Mandating more hours in the school day, more days in the school year, or more language classes or sciences classes is not the solution to keeping kids in school. Instead, educators must figure out what is *really important* to prepare children for today's world. Then they must figure out how to get that information to students in ways that are meaningful to *them.* This means skill-based classes for some students, while others will thrive on pure academia.

What Would Rip Van Winkle Say?

There is a parody story about Rip Van Winkle waking up after his 100-year nap. He rubs his eyes and looks around him, amazed at how the world has changed. He sees airplanes, automobiles, super highways, electric light bulbs, and televisions. He feels very lost until he wanders into a school building. There he sees rows of desks in straight lines, students silently reading and answering worksheets, teachers lecturing while some students sleep or doodle on the side of their notebooks. Smiling, he comments, "I know this place. This is a school! We had these back in my day before I took my long nap."

Obviously, the situation in today's schools is not this severe. However, when compared to business and industry, schools have not kept up with the changing times. To walk into any school today, you will find computer labs with the latest technology and an *illusion* of education moving forward. Having the equipment in the room, however, does not mean that the youngsters using it see the *relevance* of *education* for their lives. Nor does it ensure that they are *learning* while sitting at that computer.

The Point . . .

Day after day, knowledge becomes more complex and needs to be continually updated. Teaching and learning methods need to be adjusted to help students connect to their world. Meanwhile, teachers have less and less time in which to prepare quality lessons and to reach out to every student. Nothing changes the fact that the more *involved* the students become in all aspects of their learning, the more successful they will become. Nor can anyone dispute that the *teacher* is the variable who helps to "connect the dots" for every student.

Defining Relevant Education

When quality teaching is connected to the interest of the individual student, the student's family, the community, the nation, and the world at large, relevance exists. It ensures that the students themselves will consider their education to be a worthwhile experience.

Relevance further supports the position that *all* students are capable and that *all* students have a right to an education that fits their abilities, needs, and desires. Relevance in this context allows for a myriad of different viewpoints rather than the ability to solve problems using only one process to get one *right* answer.

Demanding Relevant Education

In order to *know* what is relevant for today's students, educators must *ask* them again, and again, and again. Parents and community leaders must be surveyed. Foreign systems must be examined to see what is important to the welfare of the entire world, and also to consider what is working—what is successful—in education around the globe.

Time magazine, February 25, 2008, ran an article entitled "How They Do It Abroad," that discussed some of the best education systems in the world. The training for teachers in Finland, Sweden, Ireland, the Netherlands, Hong Kong, Singapore, South Korea, Japan, Australia, New Zealand, and Canada is far more extensive than in America, and is much more extensively funded by the government, not individuals. In addition, teachers are given time to interact with other teachers and to share successful ideas, viable mentorship programs, and extensive professional development time throughout the year. Furthermore, there are recognitions, compensations, and exciting challenges that keep these well-trained individuals *in* the profession.[2]

While America talks of "no child left behind," nothing is being done to truly invest in our children and the future of our country. Teacher-training institutions focus on producing scholars instead of developing skilled and effective teachers. Curriculum and course objectives without *"measure"* are deemed *unimportant* by the state, and therefore are not considered as proper school goals.

Consider the following questions:

- How does one *measure* the joyfulness of learning?
- How does one *measure* a new *desire* to come to school or to attend class?
- How does one *measure* a cooperative attitude replacing a "chip" on a student's shoulder?
- How does one *measure* an eighth grade, learning disabled student, who wants to *own* and to *read* her **first** book because of the daily stories the teacher read to her?
- How does one *measure* when a kid stands up to accept responsibility for a mistake rather than to continually blame others?
- How does one *measure* a student who helps to pick up another's dropped books, when previously he would have kicked them down the hallway?

Because some of the most important *learning* that students will experience cannot be *measured,* does **not** mean that it is not *valuable!*

Finally, in addition to asking our youth about today's education, teachers must carry an expectation for being asked by the politicians who make the laws surrounding the education system. Educators must be the experts that the leaders turn to when making educational decisions. Teachers must begin to develop an attitude of worth as a profession that has nothing to do with a paycheck. Most important is that teachers must believe they are making a difference in changing the world, one student at a time.

Real Stories: The School Board Meeting

In the middle of Anna's career, she recognized that schools were producing math and science geniuses, and computer whizzes, but these students lacked the relationship skills to interact with others and the ability to hold down jobs. The education system was missing its *human* component and was failing its students.

Following a visit to the new superintendent of schools, she was allowed to design some new classes to meet these needs. One such class was called "Topics for Teens" (TFT)—a birth-to-death class. For the birth unit, they went to the obstetrics ward of the local hospital. For the death unit, they went to a funeral home. Everything in between was discussed—friendships, human sexuality, illegal drug use and other addictions, love, decision-making, healthy and honest communication, depression, suicide. You name it. If it was a teen issue, it was covered, often with guest speakers who shared their real stories of conflict and overcoming obstacles.

If ever a class was *relevant*, it was this one! Students *wanted* to be in class. It was a course designed *for* teens and *about* teens, and for the most part, students behaved because they didn't want to miss out on anything going on in class. The "worst kids" in the school eagerly awaited this class. It was a teacher's dream. One student told Anna that even when she felt sick, she came to school for the TFT class and then decided if she was sick enough to go home.

There were no standardized tests, no requirements for graduation, simply a class that *meant something* to the teens who were enrolled in it. It may have been valued by the students, but because it didn't fall into the politics of *required* and *"important"* classes, it was at the top on the list of things "to cut" as budgets diminished and Anna was nearing retirement.

She was devastated to think that this course that was her heart and soul and joy of teaching—this course that had changed teenagers' lives and empowered them to make better choices for themselves and their world—this course was going to "retire" when she did.

It was one of the low points of Anna's entire career. But, it was soon followed by one of the high points—the students rallied together and respectfully presented themselves to the School Board.

The first student who signed up to speak was Jackson* and he said something like this, "My name is Jackson Jellnick, but everybody calls me JJ. I'm in the eighth grade and I understand that you want to eliminate the TFT class next year. I'm here to tell you why you shouldn't do that."

"When my friends found out I was going to be speaking to you, they told me that I should wear a suit and tie, so you would listen to me better. I thought about it. But, I decided no, that this is who I am. And, in TFT, I learned that who I am is okay. I always wear a t-shirt and jeans, and a baseball cap, and my fingernails are painted black. *This* is who I am, not a suit and tie . . . but, I hope you will listen to me anyway."

Jackson went on and his voice grew stronger as he listed item after item of the things he learned in Anna's class. He then closed by saying, "What nobody here knows, not even Ms. Unk, is that my father has been in jail all of my life and is going to get out soon. And, he now wants a *relationship* with me. TFT helped me to deal with a lot of years of anger, and is now helping me to figure out how to deal with my dad."

"More important," he continued, "my brother is three years younger than me. I want *him* to be able to take this class. Please don't cut it out!"

Some people were in tears, and for others, there were cheers. Jackson had made his point.

Following Jackson's lead, student after student approached the microphone to speak, each sharing their personal reasons for wanting the class to continue. Soon parents joined the ranks, indicating new family discussions, and the positive changes they had seen in their children as a result of the TFT class. It was a huge testimony to educational *relevance.*

The school board approved the continuation of the class, and Anna went home, never more proud of her students than at that moment.

*not his real name.

Not everyone can teach a class on teenage issues, nor does everyone want to teach such content. But, every teacher can make sure that the lessons they are presenting to their students can, in some way, connect them to the real world. They must be relevant!

Chapter 9 Thought Starters

1. What are the dropout rates in your school district? How do they compare to the nationwide figures? What reasons might there be for higher or lower dropout rates in your district?

2. Have you identified all of your at-risk students? What is your strategy for keeping them in school and off the "corners" of your city?

3. How do you stay on top of students' needs, keeping your subject matter and classroom atmosphere relevant?

Chapter 10

Every Student Needs *Rigor*

Standards are neither high nor low.
They are either appropriate or inappropriate.
When we lower our standards,
we insult our students.
—Unknown

Educational Rigor in the Nineteenth Century

Society had a different mindset back in our early history. People had a very strong work ethic—they worked hard for very little money. They often would barter or trade a skill for a ham or a chicken. Their reality was that "only the strong would survive." This inner and outer strength was highly valued in the agricultural society of that century.

Often, there wasn't much wealth, yet most people took great pride in the work that they did. And, so it was with schoolwork. There was a lot to learn, and it was *expected* that students would do their *best*, not simply scrape by while doing a minimum of effort. There was a direct relationship between output and results.

It is doubtful that many adults today could pass the completion examination for a sixth grader in the late 1800s. However, this does not mean that students necessarily *learned* more . . . rather, they *memorized* more.

The Misconception of Rigor

A misconception often exists in the definition and understanding of the term *rigor,* as it applies to classroom teaching and the school curriculum. People polled inside and outside of the field of education mostly believed *rigor* to be more in-depth course work and an increase in the *quantity* of concepts presented. Unfortunately, when educators implement this particular definition of rigor, three things might happen and only one of them is positive:

1. Students considered to be "high level achievers" tend to accept the challenge, and a positive experience results for both the teacher and the student.
2. Students who are achieving at "average" or "low levels" are set up for frustration and/or failure.
3. The time available for student-teacher examination and discussion of concepts is limited, jeopardizing the understanding of the ideas being taught. Students don't have the opportunity to question or address concerns about a given concept and how it may relate to their world.

A rigorous curricula should not be for only the high-achieving students who are taking science and math courses. A rigorous approach to teaching is critical for *all students regardless of race, ethnicity, gender, socio-economic level, ability, or disability status.* All students need and will benefit from an academically rigorous curriculum in order to be equipped for productive work and civic life.

> *We must view young people not as empty bottles to be filled,*
> *but as candles to be lit.*
> —Robert H. Shaffer

Defining Rigor—What it isn't

Because so often there is a misconception of rigor in education, the first discussion will be to define what rigor is *not.* As previously stated, rigor is not merely implementing higher-level, more in-depth courses into the curriculum of the high achieving or college-bound students. In dealing with education honestly, teachers recognize that not all students are meant to go to college. Many have talents in other areas such as carpentry, plumbing, food service, auto mechanics, clothing construction, and various other areas of critical importance to society. Many of these trades may require training beyond high school, but do not require a four-year college education.

Nevertheless, in examining most high school curricula and graduation requirements, one can easily see that the focus is on the college-bound student. Requirements for math, science, and foreign language are continually increasing to "keep up with the world market." The hours in the school day are lengthened, as are the days in the school year. The goal with all of this is to rigorously push all students toward these college-bound standards. Instead, it is pushing many of our students straight out the door, as our rising dropout rates indicate.

Non-college-bound students still need a rigorous program. How do educators challenge these youngsters if they do not force them to enroll in the more challenging college-bound courses? The answer to this question lies in the following definition and implementation of rigor.

Rigor—What it is

Rigor may be defined as helping students develop the capacity to understand course content that is personally and emotionally compelling. It is a key component to engaging students in the learning process. Rigor keeps students focused. Students are challenged to make their own discoveries as they apply and value their prior knowledge about a particular concept. Rigor empowers students to *learn how to learn.*

In an article written by Tammy Andrews discussing rigor, Allen Tucker defines it as "The careful, thorough, systematic and precise process of developing correct, efficient, and robust solutions to computational problems."[1]

143

Implementing Rigor

The most effective and efficient way to implement true rigor starts with analyzing current curricula, then enhancing it with more rigorous activities. By enhancing existing courses, teachers can more appropriately challenge all students and ensure that state standards are being taught.

The following is an example of how Dave taught rotation and revolution enhanced with rigor:

Subject: Astronomy
Grade Level: 7
Strategy: Simulation
Concepts: Rotation and Revolution
Class Structure: Homogeneous Groups

Note: *Vocabulary development, discussion, and guided reading have already taken place. This simulation activity was used as a reinforcing activity.*

The Challenge/Assignment: In taking part of a special scientific study, students have volunteered to live on another planet in a distant galaxy for five years. Their first job on this planet is to make a time clock (for daytime and nighttime) and to produce a yearly calendar. Students are reminded to construct a calendar keeping in mind all four seasons (summer, fall, winter, and spring).

Students will need the following important information in order to proceed:

<u>*Group 1*</u>
Location: Planet Stosh, Galaxy SKI
Rotation: 1200 minutes of 60-second durations
Revolution: 180 rotations of 1200 minutes of 60-second durations
Star: one star the same size as the Earth's sun

<u>*Group 2*</u>
Location: Planet Voichec, Galaxy SKI
Rotation: 2400 minutes of 60-second durations

Revolution: 360 rotations of 2400 minutes of 60-second durations
Star: one star the same size as the Earth's sun

Group 3
Location: Planet Stella, Galaxy SKI
Rotation: 1200 minutes of 60-second durations
Revolution: 180 rotations of 1200 minutes of 60-second durations
*Stars: **Two** stars, both the same mass as the Earth's sun, Stella figure eights around both stars. All seasons will occur twice (two summers, falls, winters, springs) in each year.*

Group 4
Location: Planet Agnes, Galaxy SKI
Rotation: 2400 minutes of 60-second durations
Revolution: 360 rotations of 2400 minutes of 60-second durations
*Stars: **Two** stars, Star A is exactly twice the mass of Star B. Agnes figure eights around both stars. All seasons will occur twice (two summers, falls, winters, springs) but because of the difference in mass of its stars, Agnes' two cycles of seasons will not be equal.*

Students are expected to design a clock on the construction board supplied to their group, and to make up a calendar of the year with a seasonal theme in mind for each month. Students are encouraged to be creative in naming the months, as no "earth terms" for months will be acceptable. If a group wishes to assign a meaning to the name of each month, and this meaning makes sense to the theme of this project, the earned grade will be "magnified."

Students are reminded to make the days equal, or as close to equal as possible for each month. Days must also have time frames.

The teacher will be circulating the class to observe each group and lend assistance, if needed. Students will have two class periods to complete this assignment. Work not completed in class must be done for homework. Students should be ready to present their clock and calendar to the class on Wednesday at the beginning of the class period.

At this time, students were then dispersed to their groups in a homogeneous manner, acknowledging the fact that rigor is different for each student. The lower-achieving students were assigned the planet "Stosh" and the higher-achieving students were assigned "Agnes." This allowed the teacher to challenge each student at his/her learning level.

In the above lesson, there was an obvious rigor differential for each group. However, expectations for each group were appropriate to their ability. As previously mentioned, fairness is not treating everyone the same, fairness is putting all students in a position where they can be successful. Even though the groups had different levels of rigor, the concepts taught, rotation and revolution, were not compromised. The level of rigor was appropriate for each group. This was just one example of how a teacher could level an uneven playing field of learning readiness and yet maintain rigor in his teaching.

Note that this lesson was created from an existing curriculum. Nothing additional was purchased to enhance rigor in this classroom.

The students loved this assignment. Each group was proud to present their project to the class. The science teacher also involved the math, language arts, and art departments in this undertaking. The math teacher helped the students with mathematical considerations and calculations. The language arts teacher used this project to deliver an informative presentation. And, the art teacher helped students to design photogenic calendars. This kind of integration opened doors and allowed for students with different strengths to be able to shine.

Real Stories: A Match Made In Heaven

A single middle school building housed several special education classrooms for the entire school district, including the TMI, trainable mentally impaired, some with ability and skills of a three- or four-year-old; the EI, emotionally impaired; the SEI, severely emotionally impaired, sometimes requiring a full-time police officer for student safety; and finally, LD, those students who had learning disabilities.

The TMI teacher was a phenomenal, award-winning teacher by the name of Mrs. Lane. She had high expectations for her students of every level, talking about current events, showing slides of her travels when discussing the world, as well as teaching some basic survival skills to some of her students who were very low functioning.

Probably one of her best ideas was to establish a voluntary program that matched some of her TMI youngsters with students who were SEI, and matched other special education students with those in regular education classes. Sometimes these students were "loners," or those who were somewhat isolated from their peers. This idea was a "match made in heaven."

Students who were thought to be "less" than average in most classes, found themselves to be the experts. Students who had no friends in school, suddenly became somewhat of a big brother or big sister to someone in need. Students with severe emotional problems became model citizens and heroes to someone who was far more challenged than they were. Each of them came to understand the heart and soul of their young charges. And, each of the TMI students felt a special connection with their teen mentor. It was a win-win situation and everyone involved grew in self-esteem and caring capabilities.

All of this occurred because of one innovative teacher who believed in *rigor* for *every* student. Because she expected the best, she was able to elicit successes from her students in ways they had never known possible.

The road to success is through commitment, and through the
strength to drive through that commitment when it gets hard.
And, it is going to get hard, and you're going to want to quit sometimes.
But, it will be colored by who you are and more,
who you want to be.
—Will Smith, on The Actor's Studio

Additional Thoughts

It is important that teachers introduce rigorous curriculum early on in the classroom, and it is critical that the rigorous activity is age-appropriate. Too many times, rigor has frustrated students instead of motivating them when the concepts and expectations were not age- or grade-appropriate. Rigor must also be incorporated into *every* course offered in the school curriculum in order to ensure a consistent approach and delivery to the learning process. Improving rigor entails considerably more than raising coursework requirements. Rather, the teacher's imagination and creativity should be his or her strongest assets in developing rigor in the curriculum.

As educators, it is our duty to present a kind of "tough love" to students in our classrooms—to give them some of the challenges they will face out in the real world. If teachers expect greater things and higher standards, the students will rise to the occasion.

Education is not filling a pail, but lighting a fire.
—William Butler Yeats

Chapter 10 Thought Starters

1. Have you ever considered your imagination and creativity to be your strongest assets as a teacher? If so, how do you use your assets to their fullest? If not, what can you begin to change today that would bring these things to the forefront of your classroom?

2. When considering the ability levels of your current students, how could applying a more creative approach to rigor enhance the learning experience of the brightest? Of the most challenged?

CONCLUSION

Some Final Thoughts

The Merging of the R's

Notice how all of the *R*'s are inter-related. The same advice given for respect applies to responsibility. When people are responsible, they are also respectful of one another. When teachers begin with relationship, they set the foundation for all of the *R*'s. It is almost impossible to separate them. The authors of this book have gathered and listed key concepts that worked for them over the years. Some of their ideas *didn't* work, and it is hoped that others could learn from their mistakes. There are no hard and fast rules—no absolutes—for there are many ways to accomplish tasks in the classroom. Teachers can experiment with ways that best fit their personality and fit their specific group of students within the doctrines of their school district and their community.

Those Magic Moments

Teaching is not an exact science. In fact, for many good educators, it is a series of experiments—trying out different styles of discipline, exploring various teaching strategies, or even using *gimmicks* to help create joyfulness of learning within a classroom family.

These times can be called "magic moments" and are opportunities that present themselves, seemingly out of nowhere, that allow a teacher to connect with students in a new and different way. The moments may be directly related to the class content, but in many cases they are not. And, they are probably not found in any education or methods courses, either.

Magic moments are ideas that simply *pop* into one's mind in the middle of the night or in times of desperation or brilliance. The remarkable thing is that they work!

Throughout this book, many of these moments are shared as "real stories," and teachers are encouraged to use any of these lessons in ways that might fit for them.

Every group of students is different and responds in unique ways. Times change. Youngsters change and grow during their time with us. Something that was successful on the first day of class may have lost its flavor by the last day. Perhaps in the journey through this book, there may be a "trigger" for an idea or concept that any teacher can redesign for his/her own students.

Gifts from Our Students

When we speak of gifts, we're not talking about those "favorite teacher mugs," stationary, or ceramic apples. We're referring to *moments* that can never be measured in a paycheck. Here are just a few of ours:

- Oliver* approached me after class offering to talk about grief through the eyes of a child. His mother died of breast cancer when he was eight. He brought in a video of her, plugged it in, and said to the class, "Let me introduce you to my Mom." His talk was riveting and he became the first of many student speakers that I used.
- Carla* questioned me about my Christmas plans. My mother had just died of cancer, and I told her that I wasn't up to decorating a tree as I usually did. She and her mother showed up at my house on Saturday morning with a fully decorated tree that they set up in my living room. I have never had such a beautiful tree, before, or since.
- Burt* was a student of mine in the seventh grade. One day, he asked me what my favorite food was. Potatoes! (There's no such thing as a bad potato.) Four years later, he showed up on my

doorstep with a ten-pound sack of potatoes after hearing that my mother had died.

- Owen* sat in the chair next to me in our circle of classroom seats. One day, he asked me if I had ever heard the song, "Horse With No Name." Of course I had. I grew up in the sixties. Thirty years later, I still chuckle over his next comment: "Did you ever wonder why they didn't just *name* the horse?"

- Norm* had been a student and athlete of mine in the eighth grade. At age sixteen, he got a girl pregnant and *was* using a condom. He came back to my classes for several years to talk to young teens about the consequences of thinking "it can't happen to me." That situation happened over twenty years ago and totally changed his attitude and his life. He has become an amazing young man of strong faith. I still have contact with him and regularly receive pictures of him and his family.

- Olivia* was a bright, cheerful, active, and popular young gal. From the seventh grade on to her graduation from high school, whenever she would see me in the hallway, she would shout, "Ms. Unk, I love you!" She was never shy about her appreciation, even from twenty yards away.

- Gordon* emailed me a few months ago to say, "Congratulations, Grandma!" Attached was an ultrasound picture of his first child-to-be.

* Not the students' real names.

Each time a man stands up for an ideal,
or acts to improve the lot of others,
or strikes out against injustice, he sends forth a tiny ripple of hope.
And, crossing each other from a million different centers
of energy and daring,
those ripples build a current which can tweak down
the mightiest walls of oppression and resistance.
—Robert F. Kennedy

"I've Been Down So Long, it Looks Like Up to Me"

Our society has devalued teachers for what seems like an eternity and has paid them accordingly. Everyone has gone to school, so everyone feels that it's an easy task to be a teacher. It looks so simple. We challenge anyone with that attitude to take over the job of a teacher for just one day. We think they would then discover a healthier respect for what educators do.

There is a quote that says, "Those who can't do, teach." It is a horrible put-down of the entire profession, implying that teachers can't *do* anything else so that is why they become teachers. That is far from the truth. Simply the amount of time, effort, money, and passion that goes into becoming a teacher would indicate otherwise.

There is a related story about a rich businessman at a dinner party who talks endlessly about what he makes. He turns with some distain to his host, a teacher, and asks, "What do *you* make? The teacher smiles and responds, "*I* make a *difference.*"

Many of us became educators simply because we liked youngsters; or perhaps we loved a certain classroom subject and wished to pass it on; or on a higher level, we wanted to *make a difference,* or to change the entire world. But, why did we choose *teaching* as the means to do this? It certainly wasn't because of the pay! In the 2007 Public Awareness Study mentioned earlier in this book, it was found that in their career decisions, almost 30% of teachers listed *the most important factor* as having had a teacher who really inspired them. Another 39% listed their inspirational teachers as a *major factor.*[1]

Teaching is a *calling,* and it is a profession of great value . . . perhaps it has the *highest value* of any role we play, except for that of good parenting.

This sense of worth is not about what we are doing, or what the system expects of us, or how our students score on any tests. *It is about what we expect of ourselves and how we feel about ourselves as educators that creates our value.* Are *you* the kind of teacher who will inspire your students to become teachers someday?

The hope of the world lies in what one demands,
not of others, but of oneself.
—James Baldwin

Staying Positive

It is not enough to simply present positive stories, images, and behaviors to our students. As educators we must continually challenge *all* youngsters to work to their potential. We must continually bombard them with messages of hope and determination. We must *believe* in their success for them until such time that they can believe in themselves.

Each of us is a product of *every* person and every action we have experienced. If we want our children to bloom, we must plant them in the midst of blooming things. It is the only way to offset all of the negativity and toxicity in today's world.

Real Stories: GIGO (garbage in = garbage out)— Anna's story

The term *GIGO* was coined with the invention of the computer. The idea is that the computer is only as good as the information programmed into it. Hence, if you put in "garbage," you can expect to get "garbage" in return.

I *understood* the concept, but was rudely awakened with the *experience* of it when I read a trilogy of books based on World War II (*From Here to Eternity, Thin Red Line, Whistle*).

War is hell, and many men *in* war commonly use the f-word in normal conversations to capture their experience. In the trilogy's 1500 pages of storyline, I was repeatedly exposed to this language of war (garbage in).

In addition, I am a slow reader, and tend to *live* the books that I read. I'm there. After three or four weeks of this raw language in my life, I was shocked when the vocabulary that first came to mind when I dropped a pencil, or couldn't find my lecture notes, or burned a piece of toast wasn't "shooty-darn!" (garbage out).

153

Indeed, we must surround and bombard our youth with stories and examples of *relationship, respect, responsibility, relevance,* and *rigor* on a daily basis—we must include these *five more R's* into every school day. As educators, we hold a tremendous power and responsibility in our hands—*let us plant every student amidst blooming things.*

Hope begins in the dark, the stubborn hope that if you just show up and try to do the right thing, the dawn will come. You wait and watch and work: you don't give up.
—Anne Lamott

Your Parting Thoughts

Take a few moments to reflect on the reasons why **you** became a teacher:

_____
_____
_____
_____
_____
_____
_____
_____
_____

The test of the morality of a society is what it does for its children.
—Dietrich Bonhoeffer

End Notes

Chapter 1—A Sense of Urgency

1. "The 40 Developmental Assets," Search Institute, Minneapolis, MN.
2. "Why Teachers Quit," *Teacher* Magazine, May 1, 2007.
3. National Parent/Teachers Association.
4. Michigan Association of Suicidology, State Conference, 1997.
5. Ibid.
6. National Center for Educational Statistics, 2008.
7. Lochner & Moretti, "The Effect of Education on Crime," *American Economic Review*, 2004.
8. National Eating Disorder Assoc., 2008.
9. Flesch, Rudolph, *Why Johnny Can't Read*, 2nd Ed., New York: Harper and Row, 1985.

Chapter 2—Three R's to Eight R's: What's Needed, Why Now?
No References.

Chapter 3—Building Quality Relationships with Students
1. U. S. Census Bureau, Washington, DC, May 1998.
2. Ibid.
3. National Center for Health Statistics, 2007.
4. Ibid.
5. Ibid.
6. Ibid.
7. Pruitt, Brian, *The Power of Dad*, Xulon Press, Saginaw, MI, 2008.
8. Lewis, Regina, as reported on *The View*, April 2009.
9. Ibid.
10. Archives of Pediatric and Adolescent Medicine, July 2005.
11. Kozal, Jonathan, "Education: The Shame of the Nation," Speech, Portland, OR, Sept. 30, 2005.

12. Vitto, John, *Relationship-Driven Classroom Management*, Corwin Press, Thousand Oaks, CA, 2003.

Chapter 4—Relationship Benefits for Students and Teacher
1. National Assessment of Education Progress, National PTA.
2. Morzano & Morzano, *Dimensions of Learning*, Morzano Research Library, 2007.
3. Werner & Smith, *Overcoming the Odds: High Risk Children from Birth to Adulthood*, Cornell University, 1992.
4. Resnick Robert, *Fundamentals of Physics*, John Wiley and Sons, 1997.
5. Glasser, William, *Choice Theory: A New Psychology of Personal Freedom,* Harper-Collins, 1998.
6. Unkovich, Anna, "Changing the World, One Student at a Time," *YES* Magazine, January, 2009.

Chapter 5—Three Cornerstones of Respect
1. "Why Teachers Quit," *Teacher* magazine, May 1, 2007.
2. National Center for Disease Control and Prevention, Atlanta, GA, 2007.
3. Michigan Association of Suicidology, State Conference, October 1997.
4. Goodman & Weinstein, *Playfair,* Impact Publ., San Luis Obispo, CA, 1993.
5. Canfield, Hansen, & Unkovich, *Chicken Soup for the Soul in the Classroom,* HCI, 2007.
6. www.challengeday.org
7. PBS Special "Cry for Help," April 2009.
8. Ibid.
9. Carson, Ben, *Gifted Hands,* Zondervan Publ., Grand Rapids, MI, 1990.
10. *Coach Carter*, movie, Paramount Pictures, Thomas Carter, Director, 2005.
11. Canfield, Hansen, Unkovich, *Chicken Soup for the Soul in the Classroom*, HCI, 2007.
12. Ibid.
13. Dowskin, Hale, *The Sedona Method,* Sedona Press, Sedona, AZ, 2003.

Chapter 6—Some Fundamentals of the Respectful School
1. Glenn, H. Stephen, *Developing Capable Young People*, DVD training program, www.capabilities.com, Orem, UT, 1999.

Chapter 7—Defining Responsibility: Whose Job is it?
1. Lickona, Thomas, *Educating for Character*, Bantam Books, New York, 1991.
2. Resnick, Robert, *Fundamentals of Physics*, 6th Ed., John Wiley & Sons, Hoboken, NJ, 1997.
3. Lickona, Thomas, *Educating for Character*, Bantam Books, New York, 1991.

Chapter 8—Teaching Responsibility
1. *Pursuit of Happyness,* movie, www.1mdb.com/title/tt0454921/, Sony Pictures, Gabriel Muccino, Director, August 23, 2006.
2. *Pay It Forward*, movie, Warner Bros., Mimi Leder, Director, based on the book by Catherine Ryan Hyde, Sept. 2000.
3. *101 Tools for Tolerance,* Project of the Southern Poverty Law Center, Montgomery, AL, 2000. <www.tolerance.org>

Chapter 9—Making Education Relevant
1. "Corner Kids" David Simons on **Bill Moyer's Journal**, April 2009.
2. "How They Do It Abroad," *Time* magazine, February 25, 2008.

Chapter 10—Every Student Needs Rigor
1. Andrews, Tammy, "Tips for Including Rigor in Existing Classrooms," *Strategies for Raising School Achievement*, 2001.

Conclusion—Some Final Thoughts
1. Public Awareness Study, 2007.

Appendix A

Classroom Exercises

For Relationship Building (Part Two)

1. Reverse IALAC

IALAC stands for "I am loveable and capable." It is a technique where one writes the letters **I-A-L-A-C** on a piece of paper and tears off pieces for each small or large "wound" of the day. At the end of the day, one is able to *see* how much IALAC *self* remains intact.

For this relationship-building exercise—do the *reverse* of the one listed above. In private, for each of your most "wounded" students, write a large **W** on a sheet of paper with their name attached. Each time that you do something positive to help heal their wounds, place a small Band-Aid, sticker, or post-it note to partially cover the **W**. See how long it takes to visually cover the paper **W** . . . and see if you notice any behavior changes from these students in the process.

This is simply a visual gimmick to remind you to care for some of the emotional wounds that your students carry into your classroom.

2. Heroes

Ask students to write a list of their heroes. Discuss: What attributes qualify someone to be a hero? Or, have students write a paper, give a speech, or make a classroom bulletin board about their heroes. (A hero need not be anyone famous . . . in fact, it is often a parent, teacher, or coach.)

3. Birds of a Feather . . .

Have students make a list of all of the people with whom they spend any amount of time. Go back over the list, putting a (+) next to anyone positive and a (-) next to those who have a negative effect. Look for patterns. Discuss: Are "friends" bringing you down or holding you back? What would happen if you spent less time with the negatives on your list? More time with the positives?

It has been said that we are the "average of the five people we spend the most time with." List the five people that *you* spend the most time with . . . how is that affecting who you are?

4. Happy-grams
On a regular basis, send short, positive notes to parents of the students in your class. Writing just one a day will end your teaching day on a positive note (no pun intended). Especially look for positive moments in students who are your greatest challenge.

5. Favorite Teacher, Friend, Family Member
Have students write a letter to a favorite teacher, friend, or family member, telling that person what they have done to make a difference in the student's life/world.

6. Kindness is Contagious—Pass it On
Have students brainstorm simple acts of kindness (school, home, community). Make posters promoting kindness for classroom and school. Begin a Kindness Campaign. The teacher begins by doing something extra special for three people—one in class, and two outside of school. The student receiving the special act has a week to pass it on (or pay it forward) . . . to one in class, and two outside of school. Continue this process for a month, and then report back about how it felt to give and to receive acts of kindness.

Another version of this would be to have a "Secret Santa" all year long.

Or, create a new "school holiday" that celebrates human connections. *Playfair* has some wonderful win-win games. *Challenge Day* offers many ways to get students to connect with each other in respectful ways.

For Respect (Part Three)

1. Self-Talk Leads to Self-Respect

Have students keep track of their self-talk for 24 hours. Go back through the list to determine if most of it is positive or negative. Start noticing whenever it is negative and STOP it, replacing it with a positive statement. Sometimes, wearing a rubber band on your wrist and snapping it helps to physically make the change. Mentally imagining a STOP sign or a hand gesture of STOP, also helps to stop the process.

Another version is to notice what negative statements you repeatedly say to yourself (i.e. *I can't do that. I'm not good enough. Why me?* etc) Replace the negative with positive, even if you don't believe it! It takes time to erase years of negative thinking.

2. Banish the Word "Try"

Do this demonstration by giving students the following directions:

Hold a pencil or pen in your hand.
Drop it on the desk or table in front of you.
Pick it up.
Drop it.
Pick it up.
Drop it.
Now, *try* to pick it up.
No, *try . . .*
You can either *pick up* the pencil, or *not pick up* the pencil.
There is no *"try."*

Teachers are encouraged to banish the word "try" from their vocabularies and from the classroom when it is used as an excuse or to hide the fear of doing something new or difficult.

3. Word Power

Discuss the words that show respect, and those that hurt or anger others. Discuss classroom expectations and consequences, being sure to include class input when determining consequences.

4. Backing Off the Bully

Have students role-play a typical scenario that is age-appropriate. It might be something like sneaking out, drinking, shoplifting, or any other common theme.

- ✓ When you start the role play, make it one-against-one. In other words, one person is pushing to do something while only one other is saying no.
- ✓ Repeat the role play, with one pushing but with two refusing.
- ✓ Have one pushing with four or five refusing.
- ✓ Now, reverse it so two are pushing, with only one refusing.
- ✓ Then four or five are pushing, with only one refusing.

Discuss the differences felt in pressure with each of these scenarios. Now, transfer this pattern to a bullying situation. What happens when four or five students are a unified force *against* the bully? Discuss what would happen if twenty-nine students opposed one bully?

5. Rappin' Respect

Study lyrics of pop music. Present to the class only those songs that show respect for others. Have students write a "respectful rap."

6. Respectful Role Models

Ask students to make a list of public figures (politicians, actors, musicians, etc.) who have shown blatant disrespect for others. Then write a personal letter indicating to one of these public figures, expressing how his/her blatant disrespect has provoked or influenced your students. Share the letter with your class.

Conversely, choose a person or act that you found to be particularly honorable. Write to that person and commend them for being a positive role model for youngsters. Share the letter with your class.

Keep a journal of "respectful acts" you have witnessed in other role models, or of those that you have generated.

For Responsibility (Part Four)

1. Finding Common Ground
Design a "People Hunt" for your classroom. Look at your community. Create questions similar to the ones below that focus on students' similarities, with occasional differences to add variety, and one or two that "stretch" students to find the example.

Find someone who has spent all of his/her life living in this town. _____
Find someone who was born in the same birth month as you. _____
Find someone who loves dogs. _____
Find someone who loves math. _____
Find someone who was born in another country. _____
Find someone who _____.
Find someone who _____.
Find someone who _____.
Find someone who _____.
Find someone who _____.

It is best to have 20-25 items on the list, so that students have to make an effort to talk to almost everyone in the class.

Another way to do this is to formulate the questions into little boxes on a "Bingo Board," creating a "People Bingo" game. As with Bingo, the game is won by finding people for an entire row of squares, vertically, horizontally, or diagonally.

2. Whose Job is It?
Have students list typical responsibilities at home and at school for their age group. Next to each responsibility, list the consequences for failure to follow though. Then discuss what happens when adults don't consistently enforce the consequences.

3. Taking 100% Responsibility for Your Life
Life consists of excuses or results. Eliminate excuses.

Have students choose one small area of their lives where they can practice taking 100% responsibility for their thoughts, actions, and consequences (making bed daily, drinking eight glasses of water a day, completing all math homework before TV time, etc). Build on these little things, and report on successes weekly.

No exceptions. Don't give yourself the opportunity to back out. Make the commitment 100%. The first "exception" leads to another, and another, and ultimately giving up on your goal.

Have a poster contest promoting 100% responsibility.

Have a "penny jar" (or nickel or dime) for every time an excuse is given. Donate to a charity.

4.   E + R = O (Event plus your Response equals the Outcome)
Results don't lie. Look at the outcomes in your life. Are they what you want them to be? If not, keep changing the R (your response) until you get the O (outcome) that you desire.

5.   Responsibility to Others: Being of Service
Being of service to others feels good, but it is also a social obligation of living in a community or of being in a school family. Find ways for students to be responsible **to others.** (Suggestions: clean the hallways/cafeteria/schoolyard of litter, read stories to youngsters/elders, start a toy/food/blanket/coat drive to help those in need, become a "dog-walker" for a nearby shelter, etc.)

For Relevance and Rigor (Part Five)

1.   Evaluations Tell All
Design questions and/or checklists to present to students on at least three separate occasions to assess classroom time together.

- On the first day of class:
  what do you want from the class?
  why are you here?
  what content interests you the most?
  what would it take to make this your best class ever?

- Four to six weeks into the class:
  how is this class going so far?
  is there anything specific that you need at this time?
  what is most appealing about the class for you?
  what would it take to make this your best class ever?

- On the last day of class:
  how did you feel about the class in its entirety?
  what did you especially enjoy?
  what would you like to see changed?
  what would make this the best class ever for a friend to take?

- On each periodic assessment, ask:
  do you think that I care about you as a person?
  on a scale of 1-10, how would you rank me as a teacher?
  what would it take to make it a 10?

Perhaps this assessment could be designed with a 1-10 ranking of the typical responses of students, with some open-ended areas of reflection, and always an assurance of *anonymity* in their responses.

Educators can set up this evaluative tool in a variety of ways. What is most important is to *use* the responses to create *relevance* for students. They must *see* some evidence that teachers are listening to what they are saying and that teachers care enough to make their education a quality experience.

2. The Power of Quotations
Gather quotes that are relevant to your content. Post one-a-day for students to copy into a notebook, or personally designed art-book.

Or, have students bring their favorite quotes to share (one student per day, or post student quotes on a classroom bulletin board, or make into a poster to display throughout the school).

Here are a few of our favorites that relate to the 5 R's:

You cannot change the circumstances, the seasons, or the wind, but you can change yourself.
Jim Rohn

Whatever the mind can conceive and believe, it can achieve.
Napolean Hill

The man who makes no mistakes is the man who never does anything.
Theodore Roosevelt

You can't hire someone else to do your push-ups for you.
Jim Rohn

It's not the will to win that matters—everyone has that. It's the will to prepare to win that matters.
Paul "Bear" Bryant

3. Rigor for Everyone
Do some on-line research regarding famous people who have overcome various learning disabilities. Or assign students to investigate these celebrities. Were each of these people challenged to the best of their ability, or were they treated as "less than able," with less expected of them? What allowed them to overcome their disability and to move on to a highly successful life?

Your list might include: Winston Churchill, Walt Disney, Whoopie Goldberg, Charles Schwab, Ted Turner, Henry Winkler, Harrison Ford, John Lennon, Thomas Edison, Gustave Flaubert, Cher, Leonardo DaVinci, Jay Leno, Pete Wright (special education attorney), Quinn Bradlee (a young man with multiple disabilities who wrote a book about his experiences entitled, *A Different Life*).

What can educators and students learn from these success stories?

4. Dreams to Goals: Making It Happen
Dreams are wishes . . . goals are specific and have deadlines.

- Have students list 100 things they want to *be, do,* or ***have*** in their lives.
- Choose the 3 (or 5 or 10) that are most important. Write them in SMART goal format
  (**S**pecific, **M**easurable, **A**ction-oriented, **R**ealistic, **T**ime-limited). See Appendix B for a sample assignment.
- Cut out pictures that represent each of these goals, and make this collection of pictures into a goal poster to view every day.

The mind sees in pictures, not in words. Putting written goals into picture-format, allows the brain to *see* it as possible or probable. Another version would be to place these goals on a life-line (e.g., a time-line for your life).

Research John Goddard and the list of goals he created at age 15 . . . he has completed most of the things on this extraordinary list!

5. Explore Your Life Purpose
Spend time examining what you were put on this earth to do. When you know this, and operate from it, you will live in joy and inner peace.

Sound overwhelming? It doesn't have to be. Make it fun. Keep it simple. Change it as needed. (i.e., to make people happy, to empower others, to create music that brings joy to others, to be a leader, to protect the environment, etc.) For Andrew Carnegie, once one of the richest people in the world, it was: "Spend the first half of my life making as much money as I can and the second half, giving it all away."

Anna's current mission: "To inspire those who seek to make the world a better place."

Dave's current mission: "To help educators better prepare and develop our country's most precious resource—our children—so that they will flourish emotionally, socially, spiritually, and academically in the complexity of their future world."

- Your purpose is unique to you, and inspires you to be the best "you" that you can be.
- Your purpose directs your life.
- Your purpose is tied to your passion (what things make you feel most happy and alive?).
- Your purpose reflects your unique qualities or talents.
- Your purpose shapes the character of who you are.
- Your purpose reflects your core values (i.e. truth, trust, respect, joy, justice, etc).

- When you are living your purpose, you are doing what you love, what you are good at, and what you feel is important.
- When you are living in your purpose, you will often find yourself doing *more* than what others expect of you.

There are formulas to help you with this process. Take some time to explore this important aspect of life.

Appendix B

Sample Goal-Setting Book/Poster Project

Choose three of your most important goals.

Write each goal in S.M.A.R.T. format.

> **S** = **S**pecific. State exactly what you want.
>
> **M** = **M**easurable. Tell how you will know you have achieved it (How much? How far? Can you see it?)
>
> **A** = **A**ction (What can you do in the next 24 hours to start your goal? In a week? In a month?)
>
> **R** = **R**ealistic (Is this real for you? How does it fit into your lifestyle? Your values?)
>
> **T** = **T**ime-limited (When will it be done? A week? A month? A year? By the time you are age 30?)

Show at least one picture representing each goal. Make sure that your project is NEAT.

Label each goal as: ST (short-term = less than a year)
                                         MT (medium-term = 1-3 years) OR
                                         LT (long-term = more than 3 years)

Place a * next to the goal that is your TOP priority right now.

SAMPLE GRADING SCALE FOR THE PROJECT

S.M.A.R.T format	=	**5 points for each goal**	**(15)**
Pictures	=	**1 point for each goal**	**(3)**
ST, MT, LT	=	**1 point for each goal**	**(3)**
Neatness	=	**1 point for each goal**	**(3)**
Top priority (*)	=	**1 point for the project**	**(1)**
TOTAL	=	**25 points**	**(25)**

YOUR NAME _____ **POINTS** _____

Dave Opalewski has been a professional educator since 1972. He did his undergraduate and graduate work at Central Michigan University and has taught at the elementary, middle, high school, and college levels. He holds several endorsements giving him a wide range of specialties in the education arena. Much of Dave's classroom experience has been dedicated to helping students enhance reading skills, including the teaching of a "functional reading science" pilot program from 1985 to 1988. He is the author of four books published by The National Center for Youth Issues, and has been published several times in professional journals. Dave currently is an instructor in the Department of Teacher Education and Professional Development at Central Michigan University. Content Area Literacy is one of his many special topics, as well as Grief and Bereavement, Adolescent Suicide Prevention, Depression Education, and behavior issues such as ADD, ADHD, Oppositional Defiant Disorder, and Conduct Disorder. Dave is President of Grief Recovery Inc. and is the recipient of "the 2010-11 First Year Advocate Award" for helping college freshmen adjust academically, socially, and emotionally to college life. Dave is an avid reader who loves football and baseball and working out in the gym. He lives in Saginaw, Michigan with his wife Debbie, and they have three adult children: Jeff, Andy, and Jenny. He can be reached at (989) 249-4362 or griefrecoveryinc@gmail.com His website is www. griefrecovery.ws

Anna Unkovich is a dedicated teacher and trainer who has committed her life to changing the world, one student at a time. She has 40 years of teaching experience at the middle school, high school, and college levels in Michigan and California, with frequent success talks to elementary students. She is the recipient of multiple local, and national teaching awards, including six times having been awarded *Who's Who Among American Teachers*. Receiving her B.S. in Education, and her M.A. degrees from Central Michigan University, Anna designed and taught classes covering a wide variety of personal growth issues. Classroom topics ranged from birth to death, and were focused on goal setting, positive thinking, happiness, creativity, personal health, and success. She was an Op Ed columnist on educational issues with the *Midland Daily News* for two years: *"Classroom With A View."* Additionally, she co-authored a three-volume curriculum guide for teachers entitled, **Chicken Soup for the Soul in the Classroom**, and a recent e-book of tips and stories for educators titled, **Magic Moments: This Worked for Me.** Currently, she is the Education Director of the *Pay It Forward Foundation,* in a volunteer position. A sought-after speaker and presenter, and a very involved community member, Anna occasionally takes some time to read, write, curl up with her husband, Don Dirkse, and her cats. You may also find her taking a leisurely walk on the beach or a ride on her motorcycle near her home on the Central Coast of California. She may be reached at (805) 474-1310 or annaunkovich@gmail.com Her website is www. annaunkovich.com